D0580483

# Beginner's guide to animation

CALGARY PUBLIC LIBRARY

JAN - - 2009

# Beginner's
## guide to
# animation

Mary Murphy

WATSON-GUPTILL PUBLICATIONS/NEW YORK

# Contents

A QUARTO BOOK
Copyright © 2008 Quarto Inc.

First published in the United States in 2008 by
Watson-Guptill Publications, Nielsen Business Media,
a division of The Nielsen Company
770 Broadway
New York, NY 10003
www.watsonguptill.com

Library of Congress Catalog Card Number:
2008931646

ISBN-13: 978-0-8230-9922-1
ISBN-10: 0-8230-9922-9

All rights reserved. No part of this publication may be
reproduced or used in any form or by any means—
graphic, electronic, or mechanical, including
photography, recording, taping, or information
storage and retrieval systems—without the prior
permission of the publisher.

QUAR.BANI

Conceived, designed, and produced by
Quarto Publishing plc
The Old Brewery
6 Blundell Street
London N7 9BH

Editor: Trisha Telep
Managing Art Editor: Anna Plucinska
Designer: Louise Clements, Tania Field
Design Assistant: Saffron Stocker
Photographers: Phil Wilkins, Chris Rydelski
Illustrator: Glyn Walton
Picture Researcher: Sarah Bell
Editorial Assistant: Amy Kopecky
Proofreader: Claire Waite Brown
Indexer: Diana LeCore

Art Director: Caroline Guest
Creative Director: Moira Clinch
Publisher: Paul Carslake

Color reproduction by Sang Choy International Pte
Ltd, Singapore

Printed by Star Standard Industries (PTE) Ltd,
Singapore

1 2 3 4 5 6 7 8 9/12 11 10 09 08 07 06 05 04

# About this book

## All you need to get started in animation is contained in this book.

"Animation" can be used to describe an enormous range of activities, from pushing clay figures around on a tabletop to manipulating pixels through a sophisticated computer package. The common thread that links all forms of animation is the manner in which movement (or the illusion of movement) has been created. In a nutshell, this process involves two steps: 1) moving, modifying, or replacing an object or image, and 2) recording a frame. Perform this sequence twenty-five times and you will have created one second of animation.

Although this sounds a little time-consuming, it's also tremendous fun. Anything is possible in animation; a fish can grow wings and fly, or a teapot can wear a tutu. You are in complete control of your own world, as well as the characters you create to inhabit it.

## Section one: Setting up (pages 8–25)

The first section deals with the tools, equipment, and technology you will need in order to set up a basic home animation studio on a budget.

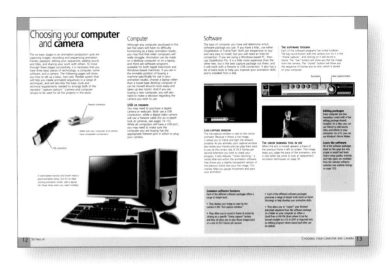

Each animation chapter is structured in a similar way. As a preview, we show how the chapter is organized below.

**Introducing the techniques:**
*The first pages of each technique section list the tools you'll need and explain how to create your artwork or characters.*

**Making it move:**
*You made the puppet, now make it move.*

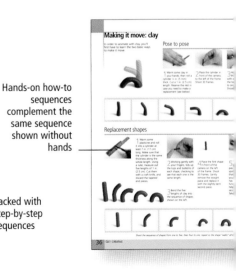

Hands-on how-to sequences complement the same sequence shown without hands

Packed with step-by-step sequences

# Section two: Get creative (pages 26–115)

This section consists of eight chapters, the first six focusing on a different traditional animation process, from hand-drawn techniques to making characters from modeling clay. Each chapter is clearly laid out and contains detailed instructions on making and shooting the artwork.

The final two chapters in this section focus on sharing your work with others—first in the form of a show reel and then as a short film.

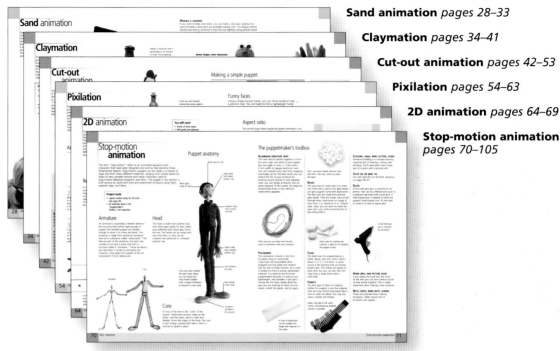

**Sand animation** *pages 28–33*

**Claymation** *pages 34–41*

**Cut-out animation** *pages 42–53*

**Pixilation** *pages 54–63*

**2D animation** *pages 64–69*

**Stop-motion animation** *pages 70–105*

## FREE STUFF

See pages 116–122 for templates and patterns.

**In camera:**
*Short, animated sequences at the end of each chapter serve as a visual guide to developing animations.*

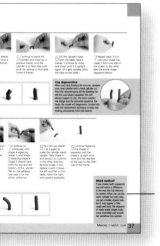

Plenty of tips drawn from the author's own experience

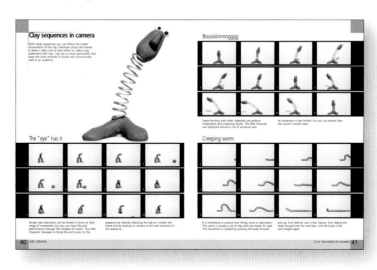

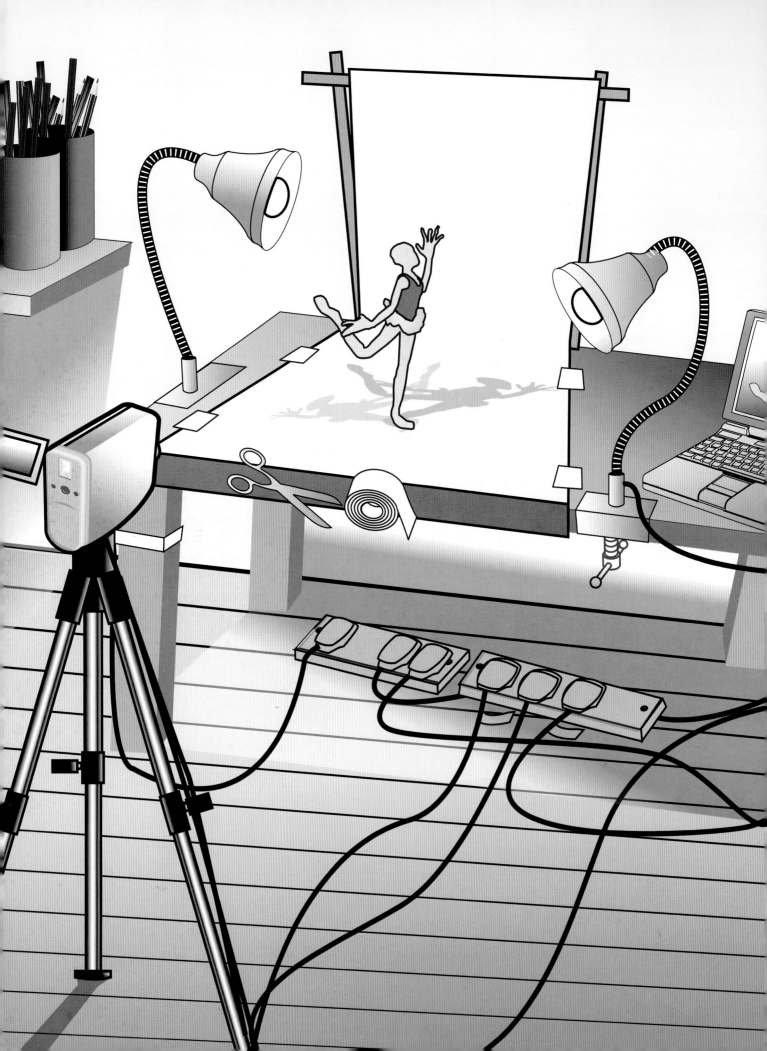

# 1 Setting up

With the right setup you can turn a space in your home into your own low-budget, do-it-yourself animation studio. Read through this section to find out what tools, equipment, and technology you'll need.

# Getting started

What does "animation" mean? If you take a video camera, point it at a moving object, and press "record," the camera will record the action and allow you to play it back for review. Animation uses exactly the same principal. The only difference is that animators create the movement between frames, rather than simply recording an object that is already moving. When they animate, they record a subject frame by frame and play those frames back at 29.5 frames per second. Here are two beginner projects to help you get started in animation.

## Making a thaumatrope

Making "camera-less" animation is a simple process and the most immediate way to begin to develop your own animation skills and style. The simplest device is the "thaumatrope," which is a very basic instrument that creates the illusion of movement.

1 Cut a disk from a circle of stiff white card stock. Punch two holes opposite one another near the edge of the circle. On one side of the disk, draw a simple shape like this goldfish.

2 On the other side of the disk, draw a related image, such as a fishbowl, upside down in relation to the goldfish on the other side.

*Sometimes the more simple animated sequences, like these changing clay shapes, are the most successful.*

# Making a flip book

Making a flip book (sometimes called a flick book or flicker book) is a great introduction to creating drawn animation. Buy a small pad of plain paper (a pad of peel-off adhesive notes is ideal). Starting on the last page, create a simple drawing in the center, toward the bottom of the page. Turn over the next page and redraw the image, modifying it slightly. Continue to redraw the image on each page with slight modifications each time, using the previous page as a guide, until you have filled the entire pad. Then, simply hold the pad with one hand and flip through the pages (from the last to first) with the other. This will show your drawings running together as an animated sequence.

*Flip books cost little and require nothing more technically challenging than a pen and a piece of paper for movement.*

*The sequence below shows a simple flip book. If you bound these pages together in the correct order, and flipped through them with your thumb, the circle shape would shrink and then explode outward to form a five-pointed star. Because there are only seven pages in this sequence, this happens very quickly. For a longer sequence, add more pages to the flip book.*

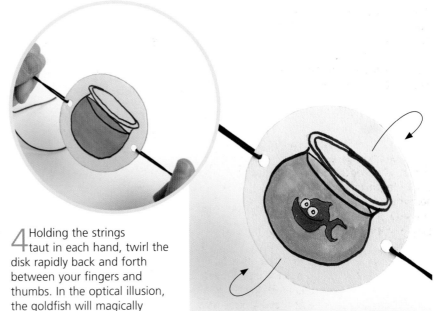

3 Thread a short length of wool or string into each hole.

4 Holding the strings taut in each hand, twirl the disk rapidly back and forth between your fingers and thumbs. In the optical illusion, the goldfish will magically appear inside the bowl.

**Next step**
The exercises on these pages are the building blocks for the more complex animation we'll be tackling in this book, which will require a little more technology. However, before you begin these more advanced exercises, you'll need to set up a camera and computer to record your images and play them back.

# Choosing your **computer** and **camera**

The six basic stages in an animation production cycle are capturing images, recording and sequencing animation frames, playback, editing your sequences, adding sound and titles, and sharing your work with others. To move through these stages successfully, it is necessary that you have three basic pieces of technology: a computer, some software, and a camera. The following pages will show you how to set up a basic, low-cost, flexible system that will help you create animated sequences in a range of techniques, and will describe the basic tools and technical requirements needed to arrange both of the standard "capture stations" (camera and computer setups) to be used for all the projects in this book.

## Computer

Although any computer purchased in the last five years will have no difficulty functioning as a basic animation studio, you may find that older computers will really struggle. Animation can be made on a desktop computer or on a laptop, and there are software programs available for both Apple Macintosh and Windows-based machines. If you are in the enviable position of buying a machine specifically for use in your animation studio, choose a laptop rather than a tower-type desktop computer (it can be moved around more easily and takes up less room). And if you are buying a new computer, you will also need to make a decision regarding the camera you wish to use.

### USB OR FIREWIRE
You may need to purchase a digital camera or webcam. Both use a USB connection, while a digital video camera will use a firewire cable (for an in-depth look at cameras, see pages 14–15). While all computers will have a USB port, you may need to make sure the computer you are buying has the appropriate firewire port in which to plug your camera.

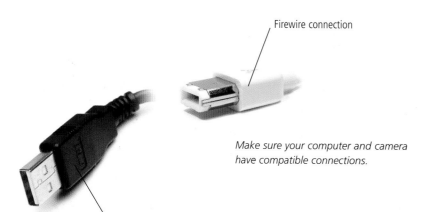

Firewire connection

USB connection

*Make sure your computer and camera have compatible connections.*

*A stand-alone monitor and tower make a good animation setup, but for an ideal working animation studio, add a laptop (for those times when you need mobility).*

# Software

The type of computer you have will determine which software package you use. If you have a Mac, use either iStopMotion or FrameThief. Both are inexpensive to buy and very easy to install, but you will need an Internet connection. If you are using a Windows-based PC, then use StopMotion Pro. It is a little more expensive than the other two, but is the best capture package out there, and it will work with a firewire or USB connection. It also has a lot of extra tools to help you improve your animation skills and is installed from a disk.

### THE SOFTWARE TOOLBAR
Each of the software programs has similar toolbars. The big round button with the camera icon on it is the "frame capture," and clicking on it will record a frame. The "live" button will show you the live image from the camera. The "stored" button will show you the sequence of frames you've shot, which is stored on your computer.

live button      frame capture button

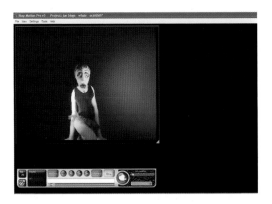

### LIVE-CAPTURE WINDOW
The live-capture window is vital to the novice animator. Because it shows a live image, it allows you to frame and light the artwork properly. As you animate, your capture window also stores your frames and can play them back to you at the correct rate of 29.5 frames per second whenever you wish to check your progress. It also features "Onion Skinning," a handy little tool within the animation software that shows you a slightly transparent version of the previous frame over your live image. This overlay helps you gauge movement and pace your animation.

### THE ONION SKINNING TOOL IN USE
When the arm is moved upward, a trace of the previous frame is left on screen. This image helps you judge the pace of the animation, and is vital when we come to look at replacement animation techniques on page 36.

### Editing packages
Every computer you buy nowadays comes with a free editing package already installed. On a Mac, you can use iMovie to add sound, titles, and effects to your animation. On a PC, you can use Window's Movie Maker.

### Learn the software
All of the software packages listed on this page are very simple to install and learn. Online setup guides, tutorials, and help topics are available from the relevant software websites (see website listings on page 123).

### Common software features
Each of the different software packages offers a range of simple tools.

• They display your image as seen by the camera in the "live-capture window."

• They allow you to record a frame of action by clicking on a specific "frame capture" button, and they all allow you to play those images back at a rate of 29.5 frames per second.

• Each of the different software packages possesses a range of simple tools (such as Onion Skinning) to help develop your animation skills.

• They allow you to "export" your finished animated sequence from the software package to a folder on your computer as either a QuickTime or AVI file (from where it can be burned straight to a CD or DVD or imported into an editing program where sound and titles can be added).

# Cameras

Choosing the right camera is an important decision, and you will need to research the many options. Look on animation capture websites to identify recommended models and types. All of this adds up to a lot of information, a bewildering range of options, and sometimes contradictory or misleading advice. This section will help you save time and hopefully make this important decision a little easier. First, you will need to make some basic decisions on camera type.

*When not being used for animation, a digital video camera can be used as a digital camera and to record video footage to tape.*

**price**: inexpensive
**connection**: USB
**software**: limited
**functions**: limited range
**image**: poor quality

### WEBCAM
Probably the most inexpensive option, this type of camera will connect to the computer via a USB cable and will only work with some of the software packages on the market. Webcams have a very limited range of functions, and the image quality is low.

*Webcams are affordable, but their resulting images are poor.*

**price**: moderate
**connection**: USB
**software**: limited
**functions**: full range
**image**: high-quality photo stills (but can be difficult to work with due to file size)

### DIGITAL CAMERA
This type of camera will take high-quality still images to a memory chip in the camera, which are then transferred to your computer via a USB cable. If you can afford a good-quality model with automatic and manual functions, you may be able to set yourself up with a decent system. However, be advised that you will have to do a fair amount of research in order to ensure the correct combination of software package and camera, because only some of the software programs will work with a digital camera—and sometimes with certain models only. Although digital cameras produce good-quality images, there are two drawbacks to using them: You can lose some of the functionality of the software program, and you can't record sequences back onto the camera.

**price**: broad range
**connection**: firewire
**software**: full range
**functions**: full range
**image**: good quality

### MINIDV OR DIGITAL VIDEO CAMERA
These are connected to your computer via a firewire cable and simply act as an eye for the capture program. They produce a high-quality image and usually have a full range of automatic and manual functions. It's recommended that you buy a camera that will take a miniDV tape, because the image quality is excellent and the cost of these cameras has dropped over the last few years. This type of camera works with all of the software options recommended in this book, takes high-quality pictures, and can be used to record finished sequences back onto a miniDV tape.

*Less expensive digital camera models run key functions on an automatic setting only, which can cause a flickering effect and loss of focus in animation.*

## MANUAL VS. AUTOMATIC

When you take a snapshot with a camera you will often leave the camera on an automatic setting. This instruction allows the camera to automatically adjust to the light in the room and find the correct level of focus in order to record a clear picture of the subject. However, in animation you do not take one snapshot but a whole series of images that play one after another at a rate of 29.5 frames per second in order to generate a sense of real movement. You need to control everything on screen, and each frame needs to be consistent in terms of light, focus, and framing. So, no matter which camera you choose, the following key functions must be available as a manual setting:

## EXPOSURE OR WHITE BALANCE

This setting controls the amount of light entering the lens and therefore the brightness of the framed image. If this function is automatic, the exposure level will shift every time your hands come into the frame (and reflect light) when adjusting your subject. This will cause some frames to be brighter than others, and the sequence will flicker badly. A manual setting allows you to choose the best level for your subject, and that value remains fixed until you physically alter it—regardless of any fluctuations of room light.

*These subjects are well lit and in sharp focus.*

## FOCUS

If you shoot animation, even flat artwork, with the focus set to automatic mode, the camera will refocus every time your hands come into shot between frames. The result is a softening of your subject every few frames, which is distracting and difficult to watch. On a manual setting, you simply establish the sharpest focus at the start of the sequence, and the camera will hold that setting throughout the sequence.

*Here is the same image with the focus at the wrong setting. Notice how the subjects are blurred and indistinct.*

*In this example, the exposure was set too high. The subjects appear overlit and bleached out.*

## ZOOM

Some high-end, live-action cameras do have an automatic zoom function, but most domestic video cameras and digital cameras have a manual setting only. The key issue is "locking" your zoom. Some cameras will reset the zoom value to zero every time the camera is switched off. This means that unless you can lock the zoom, you must animate the scene in one sitting or leave the camera switched on. You want to make sure you buy a camera that is either lockable or does not reset in terms of zoom. Do your research and ask the salesperson to walk you through the zoom function.

*Most cameras have a zoom function that helps you get closer to subjects without moving the camera.*

*Here the exposure level is set too low, causing the subjects to appear dark.*

# Getting a **grip** on **grip equipment**

Grip equipment is a term used to describe any kit that holds or supports your camera, and it is essential for shooting all types of artwork. For animation purposes, grip equipment consists of copystands and tripods.

## Copystands

For 2D flat work, you will need the camera positioned over the artwork, pointing down. The best way to do this is with a copystand.

### PROFESSIONAL COPYSTAND

You can buy a professional copystand with a specialist camera mount and lighting setup, but this is a very expensive investment and they tend to be large and heavy. It is also common to discover that the camera can only be attached with the base facing the upright section of the stand, which means that your images will appear upside down. This can be corrected with an extension arm incorporating a camera mount at one end and a clamp at the other, but this type of equipment is very expensive and will stretch your budget.

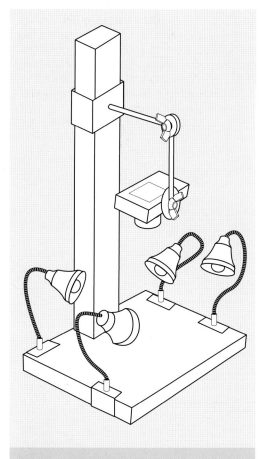

**FREE STUFF**

See pages 118–119 for a scale drawing and assembly instructions on how to make your own low-cost copystand. You will need to have the wood professionally cut, but it is then very easy to assemble using glue, a hand drill, and some screws.

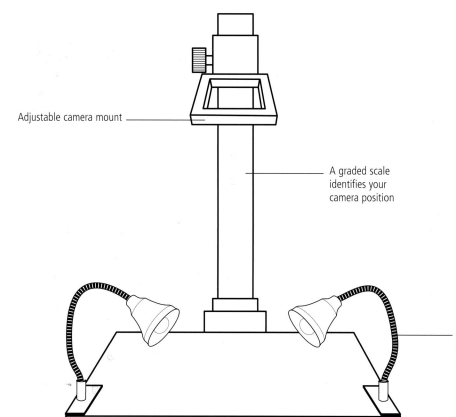

Adjustable camera mount

A graded scale identifies your camera position

A flexible lighting system allows you to eliminate shadows

# Tripods

For 3D work you will need the camera to point horizontally on the same level as the artwork. The best way to do this is with a tripod. You will need one that extends to at least 1 ft. (30 cm) higher than the table you will be shooting on. Buy the best-quality tripod you can afford. A wobbly tripod tends to shift every time you touch the camera, and this in turn leads to wobbly animation. The tripod can be weighted down with a heavy object or duct-taped down on a carpetless floor to minimize the chance of nudging it out of place. A small tabletop tripod or camera clamp can be used where space is an issue. Although you will be limited on camera angle and they can be easily nudged out of position, tripods can be very useful if you only have a small space to work in as they do not take up much floor space.

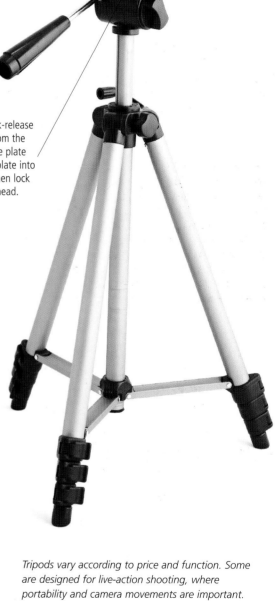

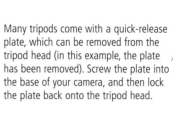

Many tripods come with a quick-release plate, which can be removed from the tripod head (in this example, the plate has been removed). Screw the plate into the base of your camera, and then lock the plate back onto the tripod head.

## BUYING A TRIPOD
You can buy from a range of tripods, from inexpensive and lightweight models sold in shops selling cameras and computer equipment, to more expensive versions sold by specialist photography suppliers.

### Using the tripod as an emergency copystand
If you are on a very tight budget, a tripod can also be used as a makeshift copystand. Simply extend the legs and place it onto the tabletop. Point the camera downward, and place the flat artwork on an angled board. The disadvantage of this setup is the awkward position of the tripod legs, because you have to reach between them to get to the artwork, and will be in constant danger of nudging the camera out of position. Using a tripod in this way also places the artwork at an uncomfortable distance away from you, making it difficult to adjust.

*Tripods vary according to price and function. Some are designed for live-action shooting, where portability and camera movements are important. Others tend to be lightweight, with geared heads for fluid camera movements. It is best to buy a good photographic tripod. They are generally more stable as they can be locked into position easily. The tripod pictured above has extendable legs and can be adjusted in a number of directions at the top to help you frame your shot.*

# Positioning your **capture station**

Once you are familiar with your camera and grip equipment, computer, and software, you will need to consider how to position all of these elements into a "capture station" that will allow you to shoot animated sequences. The projects in this book require one of two setting-up options: 1) setup for 2D flat work and 2) setup for 3D work.

## Setup for 2D flat work

In this first option, the camera is suspended above the artwork and is pointed down. The artwork is secured to the surface with tape or clamps.

> You can use this setup for:
> **project 1**: sand animation (page 28)
> **project 3**: cut-out animation (page 42)
> **project 4**: pixilation (page 54)
> **project 5**: 2D animation (page 64)

**Copystand**
This device supports your camera and provides a surface on which to place your artwork for capture.

**Duct tape**
When you are shooting 2D flat work, everything must be well attached to the tabletop to prevent your animation from jumping around from frame to frame. Use strips of duct tape to firmly secure your backgrounds to the copystand.

**Camera mount**
The mount is the part of the copystand that holds your camera. Some copystands will only allow you to attach the camera in one direction, which results in the image appearing upside down. To avoid this, see pages 118–119.

**Clamp**
The copystand will need to be attached to the table to prevent it from being shifted out of position during capture. A small g-shaped clamp (like those used on the copystand) will hold everything firmly in place.

**Capture station for flat work**
*The animation is easy to reach, the animator is sitting comfortably, the laptop is well placed, and she need only turn her head a little to see her screen's live-capture window.*

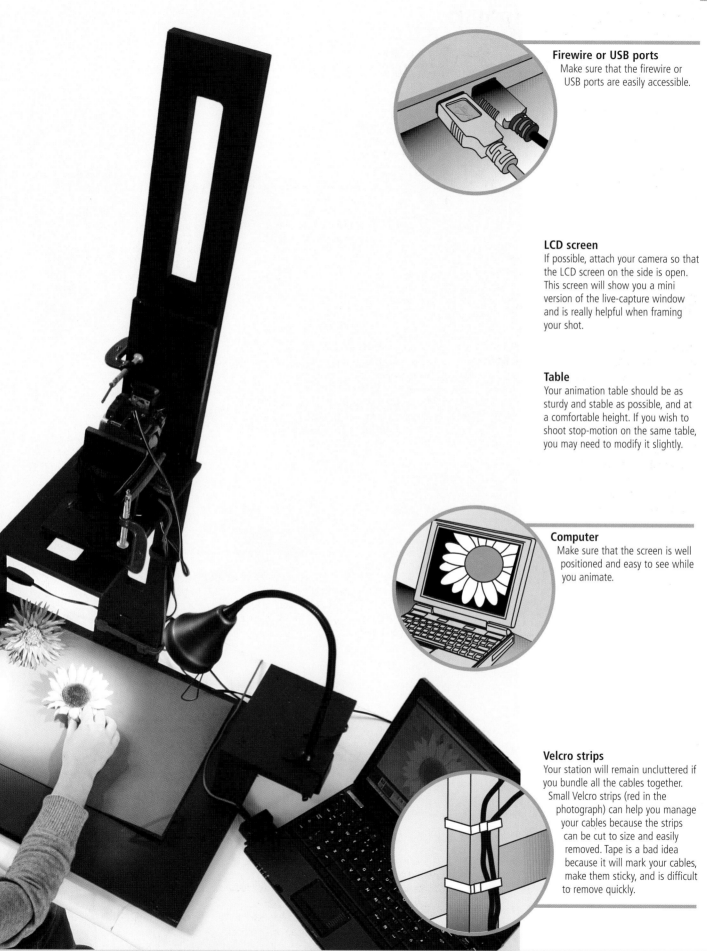

**Firewire or USB ports**
Make sure that the firewire or USB ports are easily accessible.

**LCD screen**
If possible, attach your camera so that the LCD screen on the side is open. This screen will show you a mini version of the live-capture window and is really helpful when framing your shot.

**Table**
Your animation table should be as sturdy and stable as possible, and at a comfortable height. If you wish to shoot stop-motion on the same table, you may need to modify it slightly.

**Computer**
Make sure that the screen is well positioned and easy to see while you animate.

**Velcro strips**
Your station will remain uncluttered if you bundle all the cables together. Small Velcro strips (red in the photograph) can help you manage your cables because the strips can be cut to size and easily removed. Tape is a bad idea because it will mark your cables, make them sticky, and is difficult to remove quickly.

# Setup for 3D work

In this second option, the camera is attached to a tripod and positioned to shoot across a tabletop to frame and shoot three-dimensional objects such as stop-motion puppets.

Use this setup for:
**project 2**: claymation (page 34)
**project 4**: pixilation (page 54)
**project 6**: stop-motion animation (page 70)

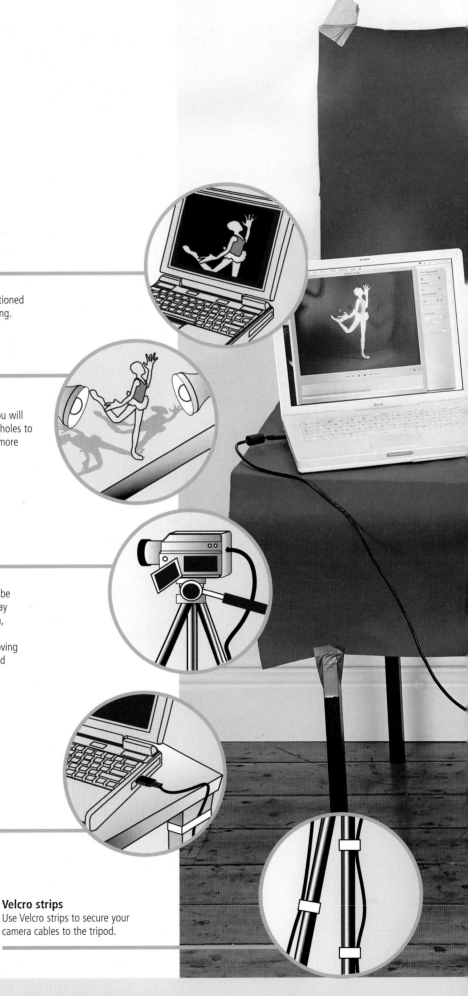

**Computer screen**
Make sure that the screen is well positioned and easy to see while you are animating.

**Tabletop**
Claymation and pixilation simply require a regular tabletop. However, if you wish to work with a stop-motion puppet, you will need to modify the table slightly, as the puppet will require holes to be drilled through the table's surface in order to stand. For more information, see page 89.

**Tripod**
This is the device that supports your camera. It will need to be as stable and secure as possible and not placed in a doorway or high-traffic area; the smallest nudge can shift the camera, causing your animated sequence to jump between frames. In order to provide enough space for you to stand while moving the object to be animated (for instance, a puppet), the tripod should be placed at a distance from the table, so that the camera can zoom in to frame the subject.

**Firewire cable**
Buy an extra-long firewire cable. Make sure that it is positioned safely to avoid becoming a safety hazard.

**Capture station for 3D work**
*The camera is set far enough back from the table that the animator can get adequate access for animating.*

**Velcro strips**
Use Velcro strips to secure your camera cables to the tripod.

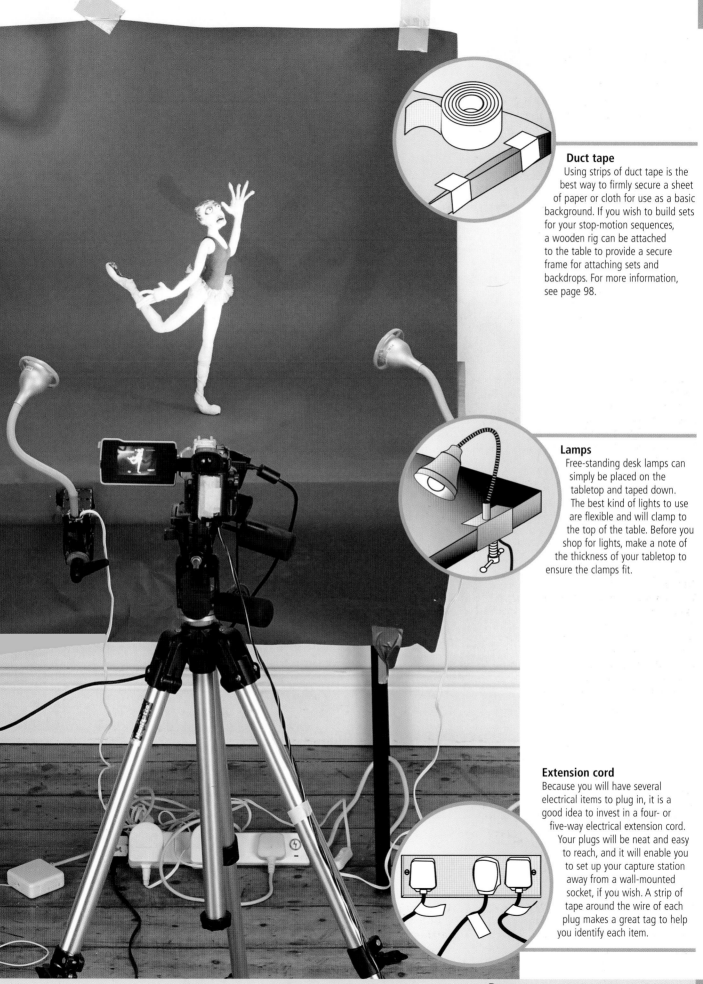

### Duct tape

Using strips of duct tape is the best way to firmly secure a sheet of paper or cloth for use as a basic background. If you wish to build sets for your stop-motion sequences, a wooden rig can be attached to the table to provide a secure frame for attaching sets and backdrops. For more information, see page 98.

### Lamps

Free-standing desk lamps can simply be placed on the tabletop and taped down. The best kind of lights to use are flexible and will clamp to the top of the table. Before you shop for lights, make a note of the thickness of your tabletop to ensure the clamps fit.

### Extension cord

Because you will have several electrical items to plug in, it is a good idea to invest in a four- or five-way electrical extension cord. Your plugs will be neat and easy to reach, and it will enable you to set up your capture station away from a wall-mounted socket, if you wish. A strip of tape around the wire of each plug makes a great tag to help you identify each item.

# Picking the right spot

Once you have experimented with your capture station and have mastered connecting the camera, you are ready to establish your home studio. Here are some tips for setting up an effective space.

## Wall clock
Mount a clock with a second hand near your capture station to keep track of timed sequences, drying times for making puppets, etc. A wall clock saves space and means less plugs and cords to trip over.

## Extra storage
If you have the space, a shelf unit is useful for holding all those tools and items you may need while shooting. This will also stop your animation table from becoming cluttered.

## Maximize your table
The table should be as sturdy as possible and at a comfortable height. If you can, remove the top and replace it with a piece of particle board. Then you can drill holes, glue fabric, and erect sets on the surface without destroying the table. Also, different sets can be constructed on various tabletops and screwed into place when needed.

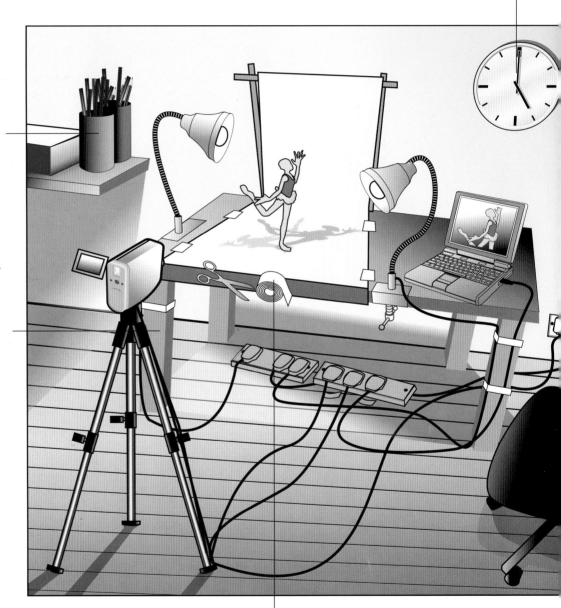

## Find your tools easily
Most hardware stores sell rolls of sticky-backed Velcro strips. Stick one strip along the edge or leg of the table, and wrap a section of the corresponding strip around your most used tools and equipment, such as tape rolls, scissors, or screwdrivers. Then they will be readily available when you need them.

**FREE STUFF**

See pages 120–121 for assembly instructions that show you how to make two tabletop sets: one indoor and one outdoor.

# Health and safety

Safety is a key issue. Whether you are animating in a professional production studio, a school classroom, or a room at home, you have a duty to care for yourself and those around you.

### Electricity
In your animation space there will be plugs and cables everywhere. Never bring liquids of any kind near your capture station. Make sure all equipment, plugs, and cables are in good condition. Switch off all your equipment when finished for the day.

### Slips, trips, and falls
Low-lit conditions coupled with tripod legs, trailing cables, and cramped space can be difficult to safely negotiate. Make sure that all cables are run over low-traffic areas and, where possible, are Velcroed to a table or tripod leg. Keep all extension cords and extra equipment safely stowed away. Never block a doorway with a tripod or a light.

### Heat and glare
Never touch the shade or bulb of a light without using something to protect your hand. Position the lamps a distance away from yourself to reduce the risk of accidental burn. Never position a light so it shines in your face.

### Care with tools
Take care with tools such as craft knives and glue guns. If you feel that any process is beyond your skill level, seek help from an experienced person. Do not use power tools, such as electric saws or sanders, unless you are qualified.

### Know your materials
Many people have allergies to certain materials, such as latex. If you are planning to work with others, make sure everyone is aware of the materials being used. Avoid paint or solvents that give off strong fumes, and protect clothes with an apron.

### Get comfortable
The animation process can mean sitting in the same position for days or even weeks, repeating the same action over and over again, so be sensible about where you place your artwork, camera, and computer. Make sure that you are comfortable and can easily reach the artwork, see the computer screen, and come and go from the room safely.

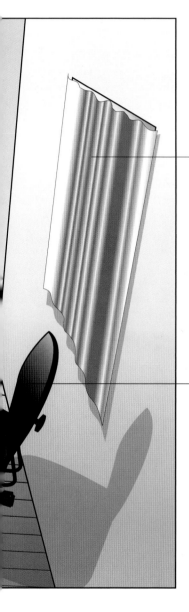

**Light control**
When animating you need to be in total control of the light levels in the room. Keep natural daylight or unwanted car headlamps out with heavy curtains pulled across the window.

**Sit comfortably**
Make sure to use a comfortable adjustable chair. You could be sitting in the same position for hours, and a good swivel chair is the animator's best friend.

# The **animator's toolbox**

Every project in this book requires a slightly different collection of basic tools and materials, and these are clearly listed at the start of each project. However, many basic tools are common to more than one technique, and some materials are used in every exercise. It is therefore useful for the novice animator to begin to build up a toolbox of generally useful tools and materials.

### The toolbox
*For storing tools, the beginner should use a sturdy toolbox with a lid and handles. If possible, choose one with a foldout tray or a section that can be lifted out (try a fishing-tackle box). Keep brushes and pens together in a smaller pencil case, and make sure that your craft knife and scissors are stored together near the top of the box.*

### Sketchbooks, pencils, pens, and markers
*For most animators, everything begins with paper and a pencil: Ideas are recorded and complex sequences are planned out as storyboards, regardless of the technique being explored. Even a dedicated puppet builder needs to design on paper before they begin. Always keep a small, hardcover, spiral-bound sketchbook on hand, as well as a variety of felt-tip markers and colored pencils.*

### Paintbrushes, sponges, and rags
*Paintbrushes of all sizes are handy for everything from painting sets for stop-motion animation to creating shapes when making a sequence in sand on a lightbox. Keep one or two small, good-quality brushes in your toolbox, plus a range of inexpensive ones in different sizes for messier tasks. Sponges and rags are useful for painting backdrops for cut-out or stop-motion sequences.*

## Sticky putty

*This is the kind of putty you use for sticking posters to the wall. When animating, use it to hold down cut-out puppets, objects for pixilation, and card backdrops. It is also great for sticking storyboards and scripts to the wall as a quick reference when animating a long scene.*

## Modeling tools

*Pages 34–40 explain the process of making animation with modeling clay. For shaping the clay, one or two plastic or wooden sculpting tools are useful when working with fine detail. However, you can also use pencils, toothpicks, and the handle of a paintbrush to shape and mark the clay. Use baby wipes to smooth the clay (and clean hands and tools).*

## Scissors, craft knives, and rulers

*Keep two or three pairs of scissors in your toolbox: one small, sharp pair of nail scissors; one large, general-purpose pair; and one good-quality pair that is only used for cutting fabric. Your craft knife should have a retractable blade for safe storage. It's a good idea to store a couple of plastic rulers in your toolbox as well.*

## Paper and card

*Always keep a supply of colored paper for creating backdrops. Roll up sheets when not in use, and recycle after use (when possible). It's wise to keep a roll of off-white, textured wallpaper on hand to use as a neutral backdrop for cut-out or puppet animation.*

## Tape

*The most important kind of tape to have is a thick roll of duct or gaffer tape (the silver kind that tears easily). This kind of tape has a million uses, from securing artwork to the table to sticking down cables (if Velcro is unavailable). A small roll of Scotch tape and a roll of masking tape are also useful.*

# 2 Get creative

Learn how to animate in all sorts of traditional hands-on media. From sand to clay to cut-outs and wire-armature puppets, the projects in this section will have you creating in no time.

# **Sand** animation

Using basic tools and simple shapes, you can create beautiful abstract sequences that look like they have been painted with light. Sand animation is a suitable technique for the complete beginner. By its very nature, it encourages you to work in basic, abstract forms, rather than in complex drawings. This simplicity tends to speed up the animation process.

### Project tools

- capture station setup for flat work (see page 18)
- lightbox
- fine, sterile sand (sold in toy and craft stores)
- 12 in. (30 cm) plastic ruler
- two or three small paintbrushes

## Lightboxes

A small lightbox is something every animator needs. It is vital to have when you begin to work with hand-drawn images, but it is also very useful when animating with sand.

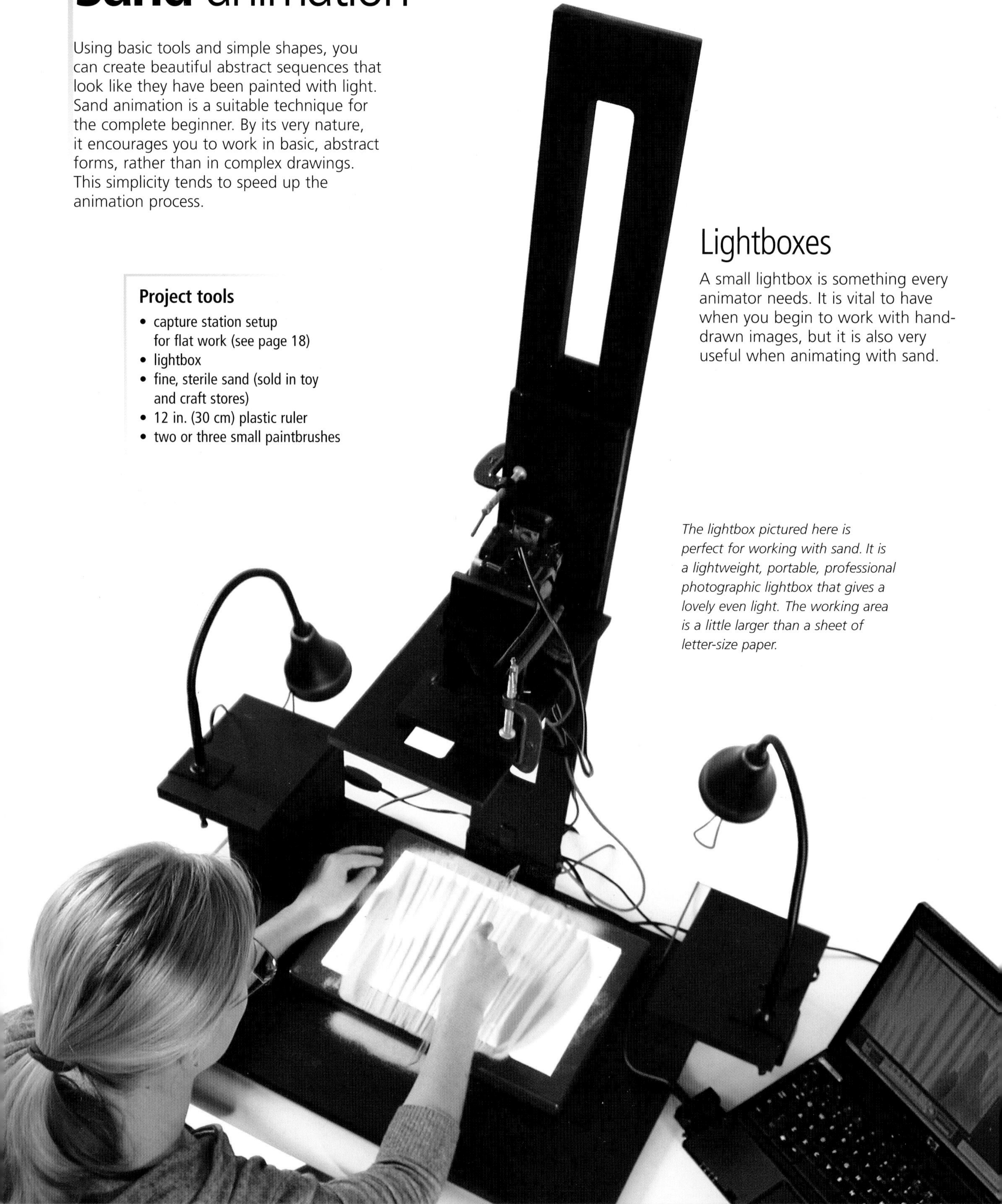

*The lightbox pictured here is perfect for working with sand. It is a lightweight, portable, professional photographic lightbox that gives a lovely even light. The working area is a little larger than a sheet of letter-size paper.*

## MAKING A LIGHTBOX

If you want to keep costs down, you can make a very basic lightbox for sand animation using items you probably already own. The diagram below teaches you how to construct a very low-cost lightbox using particle board (medium-density fiberboard) and clip-on animation lights.

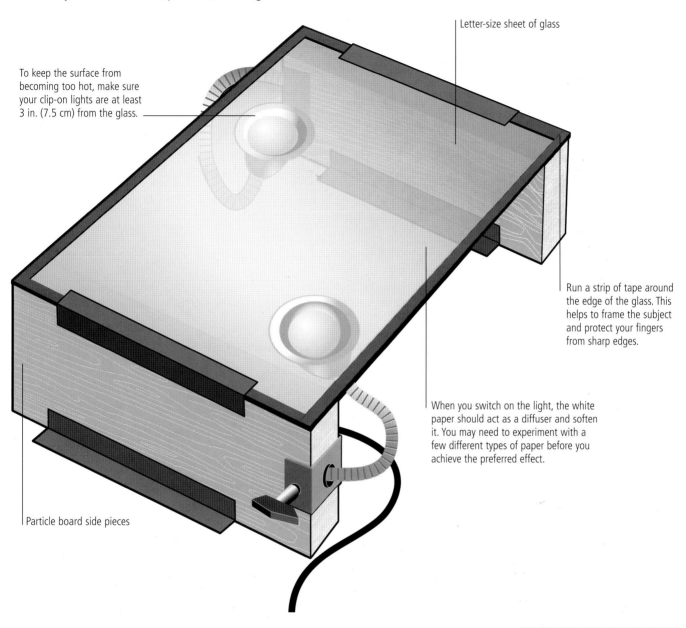

Letter-size sheet of glass

To keep the surface from becoming too hot, make sure your clip-on lights are at least 3 in. (7.5 cm) from the glass.

Run a strip of tape around the edge of the glass. This helps to frame the subject and protect your fingers from sharp edges.

When you switch on the light, the white paper should act as a diffuser and soften it. You may need to experiment with a few different types of paper before you achieve the preferred effect.

Particle board side pieces

1 Use a clear piece of glass for the top of the lightbox (a letter-size sheet of glass from a picture frame should be perfect). Make the box's side pieces with two pieces of 2 x 4-in. particleboard (5 x 10 cm) cut to fit the width of the glass (as shown in the diagram).

2 Tape the glass onto the wood so it rests on top of the thinner edges of the particle board (see diagram). The wood should also be taped to the tabletop where it sits to ensure stability.

3 Tape a piece of thin, white, letter-size paper (the same size as the glass) to the underside of the glass with small strips of tape.

4 Attach clip-on animation lights to the wood (see diagram), then curve them around underneath the glass so that they illuminate the area beneath the glass and under the area where the piece of paper is taped. (Alternatively, you can use a small fluorescent strip light.)

**TIP**
While the bulbs on this type of lightbox may cause a slightly uneven light, this should not affect you too much because of the simplicity of animating with sand.

# Making it move: sand

Sand animation is created simply by making a series of marks in the surface of the sand. By adjusting the camera's exposure, you can make the sand appear very dark. If you set the exposure at just the right setting and work in a dark room, the lightbox surface appears to glow.

## Pick-up sticks

1 Spread a layer of sand across the surface of your lightbox using the edge of the ruler.

2 When you begin to shoot, take 60 frames without making any changes to the surface of the sand. This will create a two-second pause for your audience before the animation begins.

3 Press the edge of a ruler into the sand. Wiggle it slightly from side to side. You should now see a clear line in the surface of the sand where the light shines up from below. Take 5 frames of animation.

4 Continue adding lines. Take 5 frames of animation between the creation of each new line.

5 Imprint each new line directly above the previous ones, keeping a pivot point at the right-hand side of the image.

6 Starting at the left of the image, create a new fan shape, line by line, that overlaps the first one.

7 This time, however, take only 3 frames of animation between the creation of each line. When you play the animated sequence back, you will see that it gets faster from step 6 onward because each new line is now only on screen for 3 frames, instead of 5.

8 Continue to add more lines, making more complex shapes. From time to time, vary the frame capture rate (for example, from 3 frames of animation to 5 and back again) and study the effect on the final sequence. What would happen if you shot 10 frames per line? How does that differ from 2 frames per line?

# Setting camera exposure

How you choose to set the exposure level on the camera (see page 15 for information on exposure settings) will effect the look of your sand animation. Manually adjust the levels, moving the indicator up and down on the scale, making the screen lighter or darker.

**Contrast level 1**
*If the exposure is at a high setting, the sand will be light in color and the surface of the lightbox under the camera will be white.*

**Contrast level 2**
*The subtle shift from light to dark is part of the charm of sand animation.*

**Contrast level 3**
*If the exposure is at a low setting, the sand will appear very dark—especially where it is thick—and the surface of the lightbox will appear to glow.*

Contrast level 1

Contrast level 2

Contrast level 3

# Experimenting with marks

Once you have gained confidence with shooting sand animation, experiment using different tools to create an impressive array of marks.

*Try pressing your hands into the surface of the sand (see pages 32–33).*

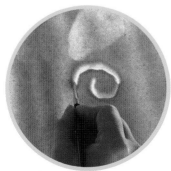

*Create swirls and squiggles with a paintbrush.*

# Sand sequences in camera

Sand animation is an impressive technique to see through the camera. Although it is extremely simple, the movements that can be created are wide-ranging and quite elegant. There is no better way for you to appreciate the movements of a sand sequence in this book than to see a strip of consecutive shots from the camera on the page.

## A line in the sand

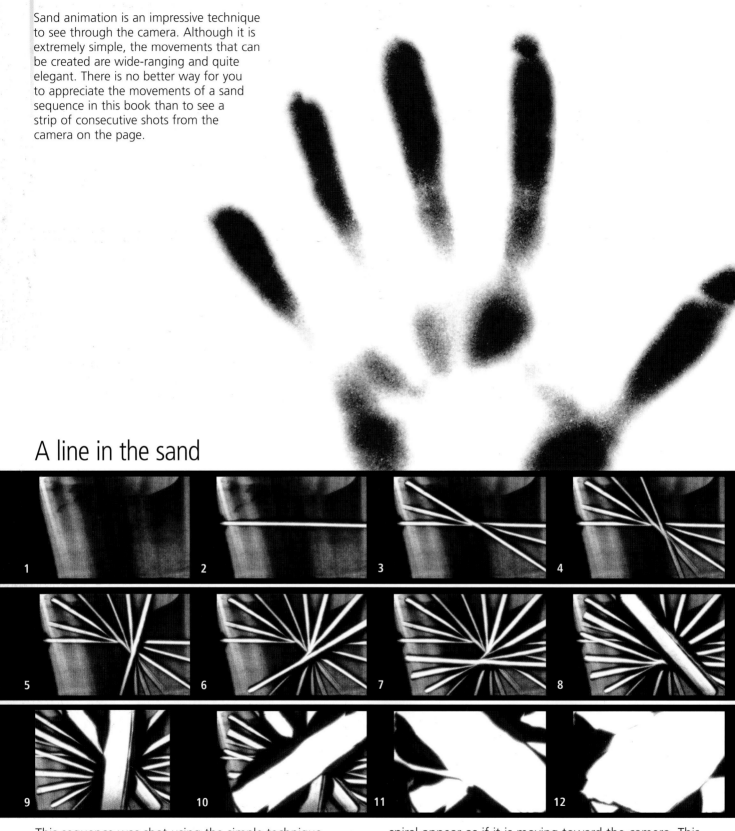

This sequence was shot using the simple technique introduced on page 30. Use the edge of a ruler to create bold lines in the sand. When played in real time, each new mark appears over the previous one, which makes the spiral appear as if it is moving toward the camera. This effect is exaggerated from frame 8, because each line starts to become thicker.

# Splitting the atom

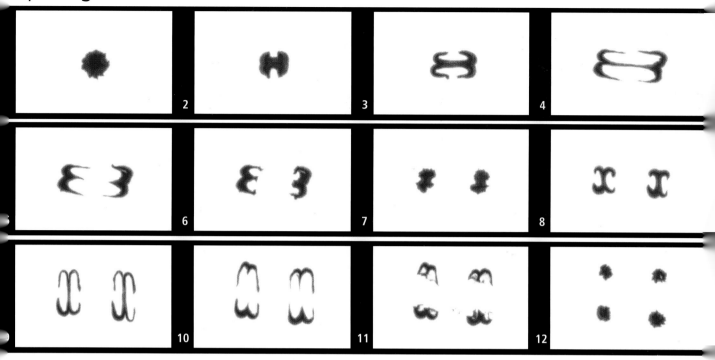

Form the initial dark spot with your sand (it will show very strongly against the white of the lightbox surface). Create the movement by gradually moving the sand across the surface of the lightbox with a fine paintbrush.

Sand animation is best for exploratory, abstract sequences like this one. Try illustrating a favorite poem in sand or giving visual expression to a piece of loved music.

# Handprints

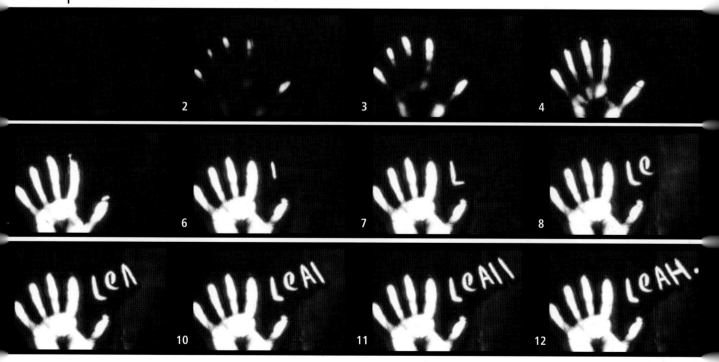

This is a great sequence to try with young children. Spread the sand very thickly onto the lightbox (it should then look completely black under the camera). Over the next 6 frames or so, press your hand gently into the surface and wiggle just a tiny amount each time. The slight movement causes the sand to be displaced over time, and the mark left by your hand will grow stronger and more defined with each frame. Finish it off by gradually signing your masterpiece over the remaining frames.

# Claymation

This chapter introduces you to stop-motion animation. Stop-motion is animation made from three-dimensional models or puppets designed and built specifically for this type of animating. Claymation is a form of stop-motion that is shot using fun, colorful character models made from soft modeling clay or plasticine.

*Design a character with a personality or an emotion in mind. This screaming character wouldn't be half as expressive if its eyes were open or if its arms were resting at its sides.*

## Project tools

- capture station setup for 3D work (see page 20)
- modeling clay or plasticine (one-color packs of four different colors initially)
- baby wipes
- plastic or wooden modeling tools (or a pencil or toothpick)
- small, white glass or plastic beads for eyes (or buttons or dried beans)

### Storing clay

*Prevent modeling clay from drying out by wrapping it in plastic wrap when not in use. Wrap each color separately to stop the clay mixing. Keep all this in a plastic tub for easy access later. Every piece of clay needs to be thoroughly collected after use because it can wind up stuck to your camera, computer cables, or even shoes.*

## Creating a basic clay character

1 Knead the clay between your palms for a few minutes to warm it up and make it soft and pliable.

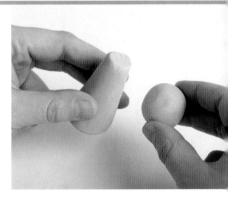

2 Roll up a few simple, one-color shapes. Here, one piece of clay is rolled into a ball, while the other is made long and cone shaped.

## Same shape, new character

*Once you get a grip on the basic technique, you can add imaginative details to give your character personality. These four different characters (right) have been constructed using one basic shape.*

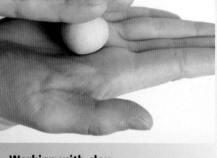

## Working with clay

When you handle clay for the first time, it can often feel stiff and crumbly. Knead it between your fingers until it becomes soft and flexible. This can take a bit of time, but the clay will behave much better on camera if it has been thoroughly warmed up and softened first.

### TIP
In the beginning, buy clay from toy stores; it's inexpensive, nontoxic, and won't stain your clothes or hands. Later you can progress to artists' clay.

3 Gently press both pieces together. Using your finger, smooth over the join between the two, blending the clay to cover the crack.

4 Any rough areas or finger marks can be smoothed down with a baby wipe.

5 Draw a simple face on your character. Use a pencil, for example, to make eye holes and a mouth.

# Making it move: clay

In order to animate with clay, you'll first have to learn the two basic ways to make it move.

## Pose to pose

1 Warm some clay in your hands, then roll a cylinder ¼ in. (5 mm) thick. Cut a 1 in. (2.5 cm) length. Reserve the rest in case you need to make a replacement (see below).

2 Place the cylinder in front of the camera, to the left of the frame. Shoot 30 frames.

3 Holding the base of the shape steady with one hand, nudge the top of the cylinder to one side slightly. Shoot 2 frames.

## Replacement shapes

1 Warm some plasticine and roll it into a cylinder at least 7 in. (17 cm) long. Make sure that the cylinder is the same thickness along the whole length. Using a ruler, measure out five lengths of 1 in. (2.5 cm). Cut them with a craft knife, and discard the tapered end pieces.

2 Working gently with your fingers, tidy up the tops and bottoms of each shape, checking to see that each one is the same length.

3 Bend the five lengths of clay into the sequence of shapes shown on the left.

4 Place the first shape in front of the camera on the left of the frame. Shoot 30 frames. Gently remove the straight piece and replace it with the slightly bent second piece.

5 Take great care to place this second piece in the same exact spot on the tabletop that the first was in. If your capture software has the Onion Skin function, use it here to help you position this second shape correctly. Take 2 frames.

*Shoot the sequence of shapes from one to five, then four to one; repeat so the shape "walks" all the way across the frame.*

4 Holding the base steady, bend the cylinder over a little more. Shoot 2 frames.

5 Continue to bend the cylinder and shoot (as in previous steps), until the cylinder is so bent that both ends are resting on the table. Shoot 4 frames.

6 Lift the cylinder's base from the table. Take 2 frames. Continue to move and shoot until it is upright again. (If it gets wobbly, press the base to the table.)

7 Repeat steps 3 to 6 until your shape has made it from one side of the screen to the other (see the entire image sequence below).

### Clay degeneration

When you have finished the exercise, compare your used cylinder with a fresh cylinder cut from the reserved piece. All the bending has left the used shape squashed. This will always happen to clay. The more complex the design and the animated sequence, the faster the model will degenerate. Combat this with the replacement technique to keep clay looking consistently fresh (see below).

6 Remove the previous shape and replace it with the third, even more bent shape. Take 2 frames.

7 Continue as previously, with shape 4 replacing shape 3, and shape 5 replacing shape 4. Shape 5 should have both the top and the bottom of the cylinder flat on the tabletop (see step 3 for the photo reference).

8 You can use shapes 1 to 4 again to make the cylinder stand upright. Take shape 4 and swing it so it points in the other direction. Remove shape 5 and replace it with 4 (keep the left end flat on the table; move the right end upward gradually).

9 Continue replacing the shapes in sequence until the shape is upright once more and has reached all the way to the other side of the frame.

### Which method?

If you review both sequences, you will notice a difference in the way the clay behaves on camera. When you use the same cylinder for every step, you get a livelier, organic look, but it may appear a little rough and jerky. The sequence of ready-made shapes looks more controlled and smooth but somehow less spirited.

# Clay techniques

When building clay characters, there are three golden rules that the animator needs to know in order to create the most effective characters.

*This character is little more than a blob of clay and a pair of beads for eyes, but it is fun to animate, and best of all, easy to remake when he gets a bit squished.*

## Golden rule 1: Keep characters simple

Keep your characters simple, and build them for stability rather than elegance. Tall, thin characters don't last long in claymation, and top-heavy designs will have you howling in frustration as they topple over at the slightest nudge. The simplest and most robust shapes will last longest and will be easiest to animate. Simple shapes can also make for the most imaginative characters.

*Because a swan travels by floating, this character is a dream to animate: Simply push it along a blue surface.*

## Golden rule 2: Keep movements basic

Don't expect your characters to behave like real people or animals. Build them with only one or two basic movements in mind. A couple of simple, effective movements are all that is needed to add personality to your characters.

*This elephant was designed with only one movement in mind: the unfurling of his trunk.*

# Golden rule 3: Use replacement shapes

If you can build in one or more replaceable elements, do so (for more on making ready-made replacement parts, see page 36). By using replacement parts, your animation will be more controlled, and you will spend less time cleaning up between frames. Replacement parts allow for effortless, fluid movement, with no rough jumps on camera.

*The sequence above was made by building one basic body and a series of separate heads, legs, and extending tails.*

## ADVANCED REPLACEMENT SHAPES

Replacement shapes can be simple (like those on pages 36–37), or they can be complex, like in this ice-skating sequence. When you have perfected your character's movement in modeling clay, make your replacement puppets durable by using a polymer clay that can be baked and hardened in a domestic oven.

*Each of these polar bears is a hard-baked, polymer clay figurine.*

## ANATOMY OF A REPLACEMENT CHARACTER

This exploded picture shows all the parts of this character that can be replaced. The head and neck will be able to poke out of the shell and raise up to have a look at the outside world. The legs will be replaced to enable a slow walk, and the tail will even be replaced so it can poke out of the back of the shell and give some animated movement to the rear as the head pops up.

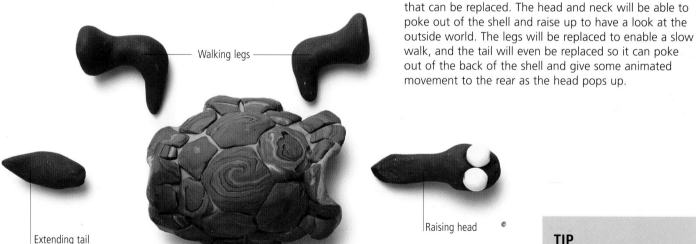

Walking legs

Extending tail

Raising head

### TIP
The Onion Skin function in capture software is useful for working with replacement shapes—it allows you to see the previous frame so you can position the new shape.

# Clay sequences in camera

With these sequences you can follow the subtle movements of the clay characters across the frames. It doesn't take a lot of extra effort to make a big statement with clay. Clay has so much personality that even the most minimal of stories will communicate well to an audience.

## The "eye" has it

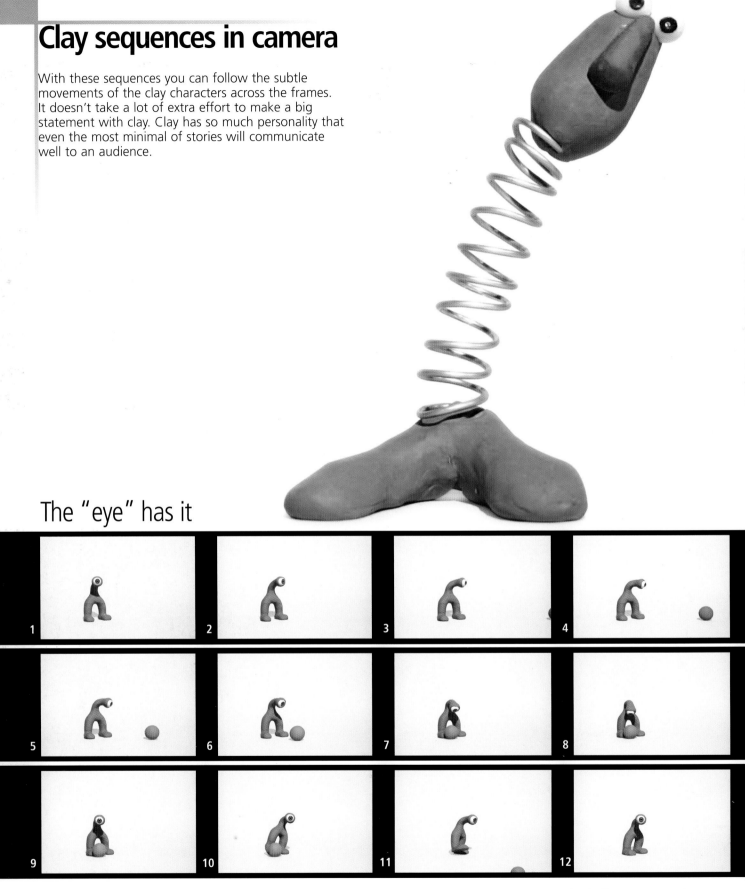

Simple clay characters can be limited in terms of their range of movement, but you can inject life and performance through the simplest of means. This little character manages to bring life and humor to this sequence by intently watching the ball as it enters the frame and by looking to camera at the start and end of the sequence.

# Boooiiiinnnngggg

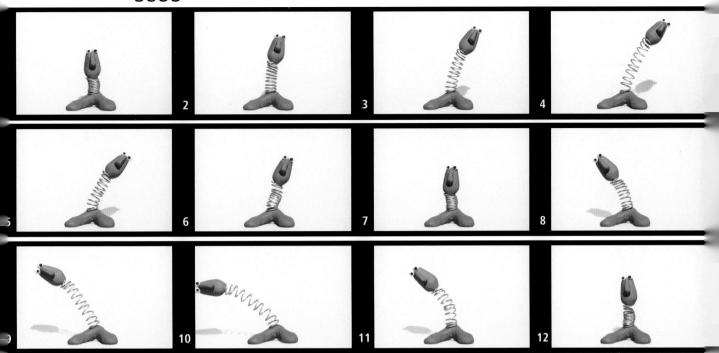

Experimenting with other materials can produce imaginative and surprising results. This little character was designed around a coil of armature wire.

Its movement is very limited, but you can almost hear the sound it would make.

# Creeping worm

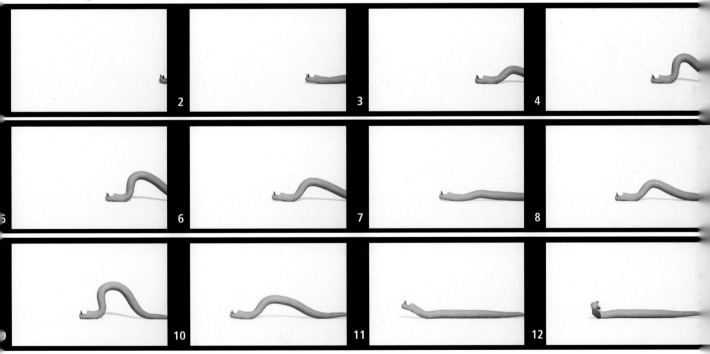

It is interesting to explore how things move in claymation. This worm is simply a coil of clay with two beads for eyes. The movement is created by pushing the body forward and up, from behind, over a few frames, then sliding the head forward over the next few, until the body is flat and straight again.

# Cut-out
## animation

One of the easiest ways to animate with a character is to use paper cut-outs that can be jointed like a doll or made from one simple shape. The animation is created by simply moving your shape a little, taking 1 frame, then moving it again, taking 1 more frame, and so on. If you enjoy working this way, you can develop the process to create more expressive and realistic sequences using a combination of manipulation and replacement methods (see variations on pages 50–51).

### Project tools
- capture station setup for flat work (see page 18)
- plain white paper for sketching
- pencil and some colored felt-tip pens
- stiff, white construction paper (not card)
- black felt-tip drawing pen
- duct tape
- medium-sized scissors
- small sewing needle, thimble, and white thread
- sticky putty
- large sheet of colored paper for background

### Make yourself a multiplane camera
The multiplane camera, or stage, is a sophisticated piece of animation equipment mainly used for cell-animation production, but it also allows cut-out animation to be filmed over several layers at once so characters can pass in front of each other.

Make your own basic multiplane camera with two sheets of acrylic and four short lengths of 2 x 4-in. (5 x 10 cm) wood or particle board cut to the same length as the acrylic sheets. Place the particle board on your copystand, beneath the camera, and place the first sheet of acrylic on top to make a simple table with the particle board supporting the acrylic at each end. Then place the next two lengths of particle board over the first two (the acrylic is now sandwiched in between them) and place the second sheet of acrylic on top.

### TIPS
• Try to complete a scene before ending the session for the day. Buildings cool overnight, and small shifts can cause the camera to move slightly, making your scene jump halfway through.
• Before you begin shooting, wash your hands with soap and water so your puppets don't become dirty and stained.

# Making a simple puppet

1 First make a few quick
sketches of your puppet
in pencil. Try to capture the
personality of the character.
Is he old or young, a hero or
a villain? These little details
will help you to design and
animate your cut-out puppet.

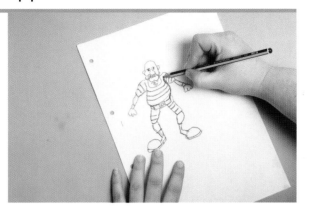

## FREE STUFF

On pages 116–117 you'll find some
designs to get you started. Simply
trace the template of your choice
onto paper or scan it into your
computer and print it out. Then
follow the instructions below.
Another way to avoid drawing is
to use photos or pictures cut from
magazines to create your puppet.
Just follow the instructions for the
puppet on these pages using the
new materials.

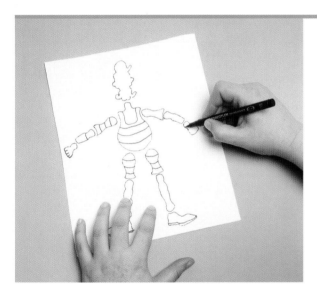

2 From that sketch, draw an
outline of the character in
pencil on the construction
paper, keeping each moving
section separate. Add some
little details, such as facial
features and stripes on the
costume. Make the arms and
legs a little longer than
necessary to compensate for
the overlap at the joints. (If
you find this a bit tricky, you
can simply trace or photocopy
the template from page 116).

3 When you are happy with
the design, trace over all
of your pencil outlines with
the black felt-tip pen.

4 Using the felt-tip pens,
color-in your puppet
and add details with strong,
bright colors.

5 Flip the page over and cover the back of the paper with strips of duct tape to strengthen the puppet.

6 Your finished template should look something like this. The ends of the arms and legs should be rounded to allow the joints to move freely (this looks better on camera).

7 Carefully cut out each section using your black pen outline as a guide.

8 Assemble the puppet on a flat surface. Decide how each section should overlap. If you look at the right leg, you will see that the upper part of the leg looks better tucked behind the body, but the lower part looks more effective overlapping the knee.

9 Now you are ready to construct your puppet. Start with the torso and upper leg. Placing the leg behind the torso, push a threaded needle through both pieces of paper, keeping to the center of the joint as much as possible.

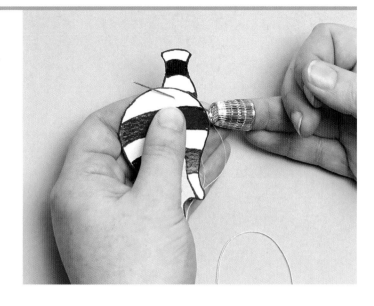

10 Move your needle slightly to the side of the first hole and push it back through both pieces of paper, flipping the puppet over. Tie a triple knot in the thread (but not too tightly, otherwise you'll make the joint stiff).

11 Trim the thread to a short length. Place a small strip of tape over the loose ends so they don't poke out from behind the puppet and show up on camera when you're animating.

12 Assemble the rest of the puppet in the same way, but do not join the head to the body (you will have more freedom of movement if it is left unattached). Experiment a little with your character before you begin to animate: Put the puppet into different positions and explore the range of movements possible. To complete the sequence on pages 46–47 you will also need to make a barbell for your puppet.

**TIP**
Paper puppets are fragile and easily damaged. When not in use, keep them in labeled envelopes pressed flat between the pages of a heavy book.

# Making it move: cut-out animation

Experimenting with cut-out animation is a good way to develop your understanding of character, movement, timing, and pace. Because you are in complete control of the design process, create the "look" of the puppet by deciding two things from the outset: What movement does the puppet need to perform? What story are you trying to tell?

## Weightlifter

Before you start, place the character onto your background in a relaxed, standing position, then frame your shot. Turn your puppet over and stick small blobs of sticky putty to the backs of his feet to hold the puppet in position. You can also put small blobs of putty on his hands and body to keep them steady in each position. Shooting in 2s, take 60 frames (to create three seconds of anticipation).

1 Holding his feet in one hand, gently nudge your character's torso downward in tiny movements, shooting 2 frames after each movement made.

2 His knees should begin to flex, as if he is squatting down to reach the weight. Begin to move his hands toward the center of the barbell.

3 Continue pushing him downward until his knees are completely bent and his hands are touching the bar. Stick his hands to the bar with the sticky putty. From this point on, you will be animating the arms and the barbell as one joined object. Shoot 60 frames of anticipation.

4 Slowly move the head upward to the highest point possible, and hold it for 40 frames to make it look as if the character is straining to lift the weight. You can have fun with the performance at this stage, and weave his head from side to side as if he is really struggling. Remember to constantly review your sequence, checking your timing and control.

5 Making much bigger movements between each frame, pull the body upward, straightening out the torso. Keep the arms straight.

**Adding expression**
Review the sequence in camera five or six times, taking note of what has worked well and what needs improvement. When you become confident with the basic lift, you can try designing some replacement elements outlined on pages 50–51 to make your characters' face expressive.

6 When the legs are straight, shoot a 60-frame hold. You can animate a little shake in his head again to show he is in trouble.

7 This next move is the trickiest shot in the sequence and must be completed within 15 to 20 frames, because in reality, this part of a lift is very fast. The best way to approach it is to remove the barbell from the shot between frames, change the hand position, then place it into shot again.

8 Flex the legs again, as if they just buckled under the heavy weight.

9 Using small movements, lift the weight as high as it will go. The whole body should gradually straighten.

10 Again, you can add to the performance by animating a little knee tremble at this point. Simply flex both joints very slightly, take 2 frames, flex them again, take 2 more, and repeat ten to fifteen times.

# Bunny hop

This puppet has been designed with one basic movement in mind: hopping. To make the jump convincing, each leg has three parts—the hip, the shin, and the foot. The puppet has been constructed with a very large hindquarters and big back legs, which can be tucked up under it when it rests. It's main objective is to appear endearing and not too realistic. Therefore, it has been designed to look simple and friendly in a cartoonish way.

1 Turn the puppet over and place small blobs of sticky putty on the tips of the ears, back foot, front foot, and nose. Place it in a "resting" position to the left of the frame, and press the feet and ears to stick them to the surface.

2 Shooting in 2s, raise its ears up over 5 frames as if the rabbit has just heard a noise.

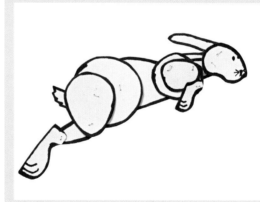

6 The back leg should now leave the ground and stretch out behind the body.

7 When the rabbit reaches the middle of the jump, its body is fully stretched out and almost level, parallel to the ground.

3 Over the next 5 frames gradually push the rabbit's head down as close to its body as it will go, while moving its ears back at the same time.

4 Leading with the head, move the front half of the body upward and slightly to the right over 3 frames.

5 Without moving the back foot, stretch the torso out and tuck the front leg up as much as possible. Then take 2 frames.

8 Its front leg should bend as it touches the ground, and its hindquarters should quickly follow.

9 Generally, an object will always fall faster than it rises; therefore, there should be less frames in the descent. Its front end should now appear lower than its back end, and its back leg should tuck up under its body.

10 As its body settles close to the ground, its ears should quickly pop back up, over 3 frames. At the same time, pull the rabbit's chest upward slightly, while pushing its hindquarters downward. This puts it in a similar position to the start frame and makes it easier to cycle the animation (see glossary, page 124) when you edit the sequence.

# Cut-out variations

Once you become familiar with the basic principles of cut-out animation, you can begin to experiment with different materials and techniques. Here are some imaginative approaches to get you started.

a

b

c      d      e

*The elements*

## REPLACEMENT ANIMATION

Sketch out a basic movement, for example, the big fish (above), opening its mouth in a three-drawing sequence. Color in each drawing and cut them out (backing the paper with duct tape first). Now, simply shoot the scene as a simple cut-out sequence, but when it is time for the little fish to be swallowed, replace the entire big fish shape between frames.

(see page 28)

## SHADOW SHAPES

Make shadow puppets with black paper, then create cut-outs in them with a craft knife. Glue pieces of colored celophane behind the cut-outs, and string the puppet together with needle and thread as usual. When placed on a lightbox (see page 28), the puppet glows. This technique is often used to illustrate folk tales.

a

a

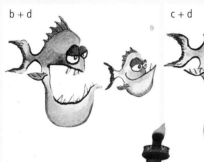
b + d

c + d

b + d

a

b + e

## SELF PORTRAIT

Using a digital stills camera, have a friend take a shot of your face against a contrasting background. Load the picture onto your computer and print it out. Flick through some old magazines or newspapers to find a "body" to go with your face (this could be a superhero, a celebrity, or a historical figure). Back both images with duct tape, cut them out, and shoot simple movements under the camera. For more ambitious sequences, shoot a number of pictures of your face in different positions (looking up, in profile, mouth open) and replace the entire head between shots.

## SEGMENTED CHARACTERS

If you join a number of disks together, you can make a character that will move in a very fluid, realistic manner. This design works especially well for snake, worm, and caterpillar puppets, but it can also be used as part of any animal design (for example, a long neck on a giraffe).

Cut out a basic face.

## ANIMATED FACES

Cut out a simple face shape but do not draw in the eyes or mouth. Design appropriate eye shapes (including closed eye shapes) and a variety of mouths, and cut them out. Create different expressions by moving and replacing the shapes between frames. You can even try basic lip sync using this technique.

*Prepare different mouths and eyes.*

*Mix and match the different mouth and eye shapes on the face.*

*Changing the position of the eyes in relation to the eyebrows gives a different expression.*

---

## BRING A PAINTING TO LIFE

**1** First, you will need to choose a portrait. One with a clearly defined facial expression is best. You will need two identical pictures, so it is advisable to print out the painting of your choice from the internet. Back both paintings with duct tape. Using the line between the upper and lower lip as a guide, cut the lower jaw from one image. Draw a set of teeth on white paper, cut them out, and glue them to a small piece of black paper.

**2** Using the line between the upper and lower lips as a guide, cut an open mouth shape from the second picture, keeping the cut-out of the jaw to one side. A small pair of white paper circles can be glued over the eyes (use small black circles for animatable pupils).

**3** Glue the teeth in position to the inside of the open mouth shape and place the lower jaw over the open mouth. By moving the jaw up and down you can make the character "speak" in a manner reminiscent of a ventriloquist's dummy. Move the pupils to simulate eye movement.

Cut-out jaw

# Cut-out sequences in camera

The best way to "see" an animated sequence in print is to show its movement frame by frame. These image sequences are all taken from short animated films. There are 12 frames in each sequence, so if you shoot in 2 frames each time you move the puppet, each sequence will last for one second. It is a good idea to shoot a 60-frame hold at the start of each sequence, as your audience will need time to "settle in" to the sequence before the movement begins. This "hold" has the advantage of adding two precious seconds to the running time!

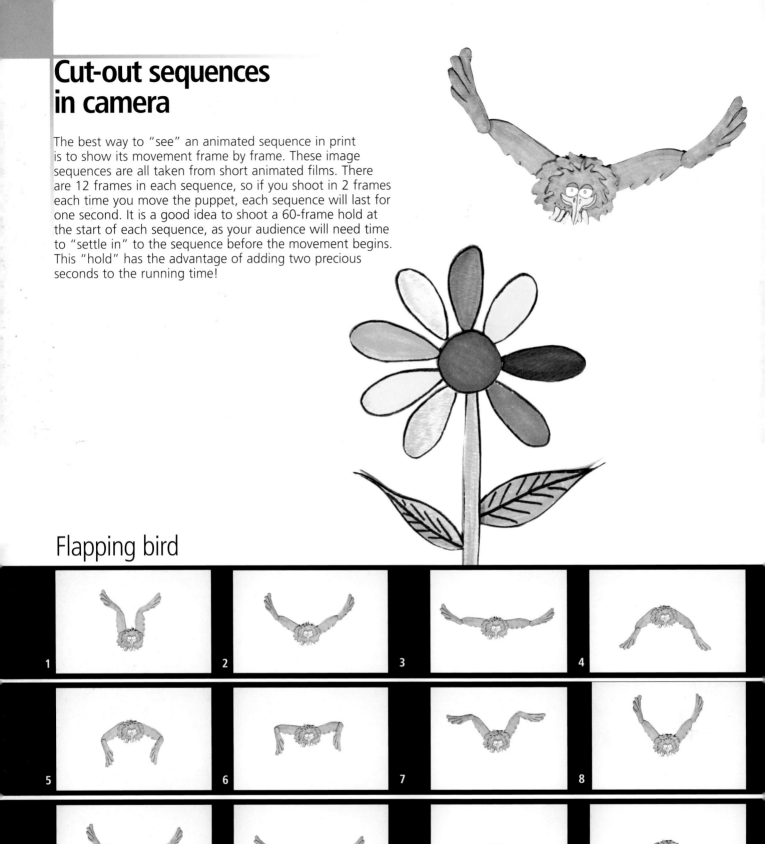

## Flapping bird

This sequence is a good example of an animated cycle, where a repeated action can be looped (see glossary, page 124). This simple puppet has been made using the technique outlined on pages 43–45 and has four joints, two in each wing.

# Flower

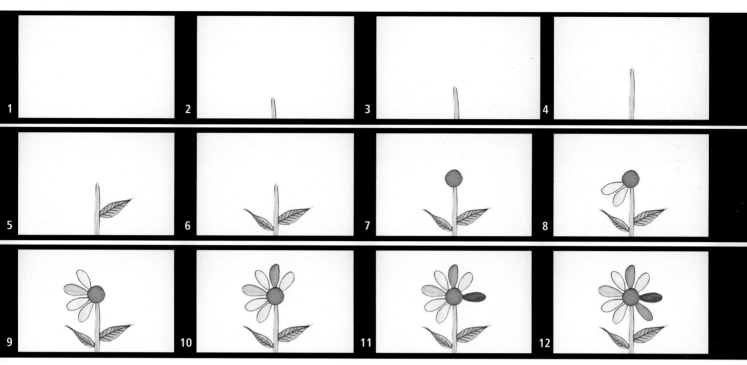

A simple image built up over a series of frames is a simple and effective exercise for the complete beginner. The only animated element here is the stem, which "grows" gradually into the frame. The flower itself is simply built by adding one petal at a time.

# Weightlifter

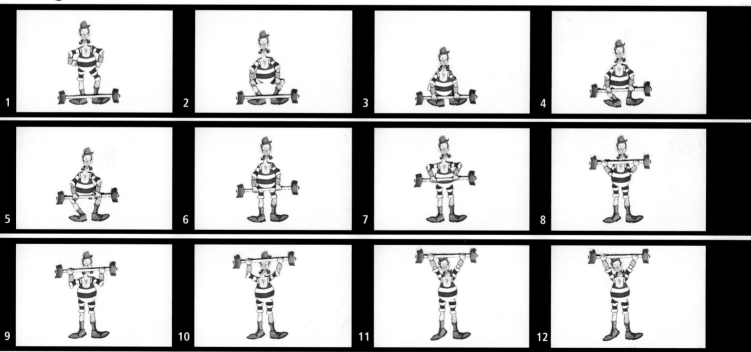

Both the flapping bird and the growing flower are quick to make and quick to animate. You will notice that it will take you a little longer to complete a more ambitious sequence, such as the weightlifting exercise above.

When you become more confident, you can design characters with a specific action in mind. The weightlifter is a good character to begin with because he has one main aim in life: to lift that weight.

# Pixilation

Pixilation animation made with real objects, such as toys, food, and even people, can be creative and fun. Collect some interesting bits and pieces with which to animate. It is best to begin with flatter objects; Coins, sweets, and matchsticks are all good starter items, but anything goes once you get the hang of the technique. A variety of textures and colors in the same shot will also make your sequence more interesting. Don't make your pixilation subject too complex, however, otherwise you will cross over into the realm of stop-motion.

*Small toys and brightly colored decorative objects can create very lively and whimsical sequences.*

## Animating with simple objects

1 Arrange your objects under the camera. Remember that before you begin to shoot it is important to spend a bit of time getting the sharpest possible image through the camera lens. Adjust your lights, and set the white balance and focus on the camera (see page 15).

2 Shooting in 2s, take a 60- to 70-frame hold (shoot the frames without moving anything to create a short pause before the animation starts. This allows your audience to take in the scene before any movement begins). To start animating, simply move the orange flower a short distance and take 2 frames. Continue to move the object gradually downward in a straight line, shooting 2 frames between each movement.

### Project tools

- capture station initially setup for flat work (see page 18), then for 3D work (see page 20) as you progress in the exercises
- collection of objects with which to animate, or some willing friends
- large sheet of colored paper to use as background
- sticky putty
- duct tape
- wooden frame with Perspex or acrylic or sheet to replace the glass (if necessary)
- fabric with face-size hole
- stiff cardboard
- sticky-back Velcro tabs
- drill
- small, square piece of particle board
- wooden barbecue skewer
- wood glue

3 When you play the sequence back, the orange flower will move from its starting position down the frame. If you made very large movements with the flower, the change of position will happen quickly, over a small number of frames. If you made very tiny movements and took a lot of frames, the flower will move more slowly.

### TIPS
- Experiment with the pace and bring the other objects into the action as you become more confident. Try spinning the objects in place, as well as moving them around the frame.
- To avoid nudging an object out of position by mistake, place a tiny blob of sticky putty on the back of each object, and press it gently into the background with each movement.

# Funny faces

Using a simple picture frame, you can shoot pixilation over a person's face. You will need to find a lightweight frame that contains Perspex or acrylic instead of glass. Secure the Perspex firmly in the frame with duct tape.

1 The subject lies down and pokes his head through a hole in a piece of fabric. In the picture (far right) the fabric is black, but you can use any color you like.

2 Rest the frame against a sturdy object placed behind the subject's head (a low coffee table or stool is ideal). The Perspex should be at least 4 in. (10 cm) away from the subject's face. Gently lower the frame into position, resting it lightly on the subject's chest.

3 The image is framed by the camera directly above the subject's head.

4 Position objects on the acrylic/Perspex sheet and animate by moving them across the surface within the frame.

## TIPS

- Make sure your subject doesn't have any back problems and is happy to lie on his or her back for a long period of time.
- Position the lights so that they are not shining directly into the subject's face.
- Provide a lot of cushions to support your subject's head and back. Give him or her time to get comfortable.

## MORE FUNNY FACES

This image was created by slicing fruit and vegetables in half and placing them on the acrylic sheet over the face using the camera view as a guide.

Paper cut-outs can have great effect. Here the pupils are dots of black paper and can be moved from side to side.

The eyebrows can also be moved to create a variety of expressions, and the mouth can be replaced by a different shape to change expression or to make a new character.

You can create a whole character using a jointed, cut-out puppet (see pages 42–45). With this technique, the acrylic or Perspex sheet and frame are unnecessary: Simply rest the cut-out on the subject's chest. By changing his or her expression, your actor can really bring the story to life.

When using the cut-out puppet technique, use a piece of stiff card under the fabric to create a level surface on which to animate. Add more details, like a hat or bag, as the story progresses—use Velcro tabs to keep objects steady on the fabric.

# Making it move: pixilation

Simply creating movement from still objects or drawings is exciting and rewarding. However, as you develop your skills, your ideas become more ambitious and start to tell more complex stories. When an object begins to take on a character and movement becomes controlled and purposeful, you will need to incorporate the two fundamental principles of pixilation animation: pace and performance.

## Follow the leader

When an animated sequence involves a group of objects randomly drifting around the frame, it can lack a certain dynamic. If you can give that group of objects a common purpose, or even imply a relationship between them, your sequence is more believable. For example, varying the pace of the group as it moves across the frame will give energy to an abstract piece.

1 On a neutral background arrange 15 to 20 jellybeans at the bottom left-hand corner of the frame. Each bean should be lightly stuck down with putty or carefully cut in half along its length to help it sit in place. Take a 60-frame hold (60 frames without moving anything).

2 Over the next 60 frames, gradually nudge each bean until they are all pointing in the same direction.

3 Over the next 20 frames, allow one bean to become the "leader" (in this case, the purple one) by moving it toward the top right corner. The other beans should follow and begin to form a wedge shape behind the leader.

## Who is that?

An audience will follow a sequence on screen more easily if the animated objects "perform" the action well. Implying a relationship between two inanimate objects can help to tell a story. Developing your performance skills will challenge you as an animator.

1 Set both lamps in a position that makes them appear to be "looking" at each other.

2 Over 10 frames turn each lamp head so that they appear to look at something just left of the frame.

3 Over the next 30 frames, introduce a ball slowly from the bottom left of the frame. The ball should continue its progress into the frame, with the lamps repositioned slightly between each frame to follow its movement.

*In animation you can make any inanimate object expressive by focusing on its performance.*

**4** Over the next 30 frames, begin to spread the group out, with the first five or six beans moving faster than the tail end of the group.

**5** As the purple bean reaches the top of the frame, begin to arrange the group in a gentle, sweeping curve.

**6** Over the next 15 frames, make the curve more pronounced as the slower beans at the back of the group catch up.

**7** Over the next 10 frames, swing the group around the leader bean, tucking it behind the purple bean in the top right-hand corner.

**8** Arrange the beans into a tight group and hold for 60 frames, maintaining a little movement by nudging each bean ever so slightly between frames. Then begin to move the beans back to the first corner, but this time, double the distance traveled by each bean to complete the journey across the frame in half the time.

**4** Pause for 20 frames, then use just 10 frames for the lamps to quickly turn to face each other. Hold the look for 50 frames. The ball can continue to move into the frame—it will move only slightly and the lamps will completely change position.

**5** Move the lamps in unison over 10 frames until they are looking down toward the ball again. Hold for 20 frames without moving the ball or the lamps.

**6** The ball should then continue its progress across the frame, with the lamps following its movement (use anything up to 100 frames). For a big comedy pause, shoot 50 frames without moving anything as the ball comes into position between the lamps.

**7** Over the next 100 to 150 frames, move the ball to the far right of the screen and then out of shot at the top right corner. The lamps should follow its movements exactly.

**8** Shoot a 40-frame hold after the ball has left the screen, then, over sixty frames, slowly turn both lamps so that they are "looking" directly at the camera. Shoot a 60-frame hold.

# Playing dress-up

1 Create a simple sequence using nothing more than a few dressmakers' pins and a shirt. Here, the subject stands in the center of the frame, holding his arms out slightly from the body. Place a colored shirt just behind him on the floor. The subject should remain as still as possible. Shoot a 40-frame hold.

2 Using the pins, carefully attach the shirt to the bottom of the jeans, making it look as if the shirt is slowly climbing up the subject's legs. The subject should maintain his position until the shirt has reached his knees. Take 8 to 10 frames to move the shirt from the floor to the subject's knees.

3 Ask the subject to start to react to the creeping shirt by hunching his shoulders and looking down in surprise. The movements between frames need to be very small, and the subject should hold each new facial position until the shot has been taken. Complete this movement in 5 or 6 frames.

4 As the shirt works its way up the body, the subject's right hand should slip into the armhole, followed shortly after by the right arm. By now, you should be securing the shirt by pinning it to the subject's own shirt. Keep the movements small. Try to stretch this action over 10 to 15 frames.

# Banana striptease

## BANANA STRIPTEASE: PREPARATION

1 Using a small drill bit, drill two holes side by side through the center of a small square of particle board.

2 Break a wooden skewer in half, and glue both pieces into the holes with the pointed ends sticking up through the tabletop.

3 Choose a background paper and cut a small hole in the bottom half (just big enough for the skewers to fit through).

4 Thread the skewers through, and gently impale a banana on them. The banana should look as if it is standing up all on its own.

5 Light and frame the banana so that the entire length is well in shot and the banana is positioned in the center of the frame.

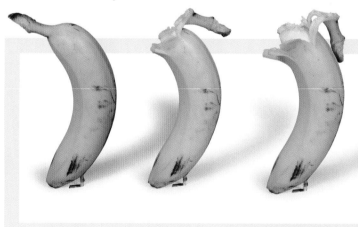

1 Shoot a 60-frame hold without any movement.

2 Hold the banana firmly with one hand and gently peel back a tiny section of peel. Shoot 2 frames.

3 Continue to peel the banana, a tiny bit at a time, shooting 2 frames between each movement.

5 When both arms are safely inside the sleeves, allow the shirt to creep slowly up the shoulders. It will help the sequence to slow the action down right here, so try to stretch this action out over 20 frames.

6 Over the next 50 frames or so, gradually settle the shirt into a final position.

7 Close the buttons one by one, shooting 5 frames on each button.

8 Your subject should now strike a pose, proudly showing off the completed ensemble. Shoot a 40-frame hold to finish off the sequence.

4 As the peeled-back sections become longer, make sure that they fall outward.

5 Keep peeling and shooting until the tips of the peel begin to touch the surface of the table.

6 Keep the loose ends of the peel under control by tucking them inward.

7 It is difficult to plan the frame rate precisely, but try to shoot the action over at least 20 frames.

# The flower

1 Position the actors so that they are facing each other. They must try to keep their arms and legs in the same position for most of the sequence, so it is important they find a comfortable pose. Just before the first frame is shot, they each lift one foot off the ground.

2 Between frames, they each take a small step toward each other, again raising their feet before the shot is taken. When the sequence is played back, it will look as if the characters are skating along the ground on one foot.

3 Continue in the same way until the characters are about 1 ft. (30 cm) apart and in the center of the frame. The number of frames you take will determine the speed and duration of the sequence: 60 frames (a little over two seconds) of movement is suggested.

**TIPS**
Plan the movement with your cast. It is important that they know exactly what you have in mind. Walk through the moves a few times, marking the floor with chalk if necessary.

4 The characters gradually lower their feet over at least 10 frames, and hold a standing position for at least 50 frames (two seconds). It is important that the flower is visible in the shot and not tucked behind the actor's body.

5 Over the next 29.5 frames (one second) the actor gradually brings the flower around to the front. Both actors hold the final position for another 30 frames. Both actors should remain still with neutral faces.

6 Over the next 20 frames, the actress slowly, and with an exaggerated facial expression, reacts happily to the surprise gift of the flower. The actor, meanwhile, breaks slowly into a smile.

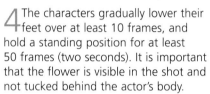

7 The actress then reaches out slowly, over at least 50 frames, and takes the flower. Note that where possible, both actors maintain the same position throughout the sequence.

8 Once the actress has taken the flower you can either continue by having the characters turn and move out of frame or simply reverse the frames in post-production and double the length of the shot.

# Pixilation sequences in camera

Pixilation is an excellent technique to try if you want to get to grips with simple timing. Once you have mastered the basics of planning and setting up pixilated scenes, you can begin to develop your animation skills and storytelling ability.

## The race

This simple sequence is really an exercise in pace. Both the bottle and the ball are initially placed in the same position to the right of the frame, and both are moved between every frame. However, the bottle is moved twice the distance covered by the ball. Therefore while the ball just about makes it to the center of the frame over the 20 frames, the bottle gets all the way to the left of the frame and back to the center over the same number of frames.

# Flower and vase

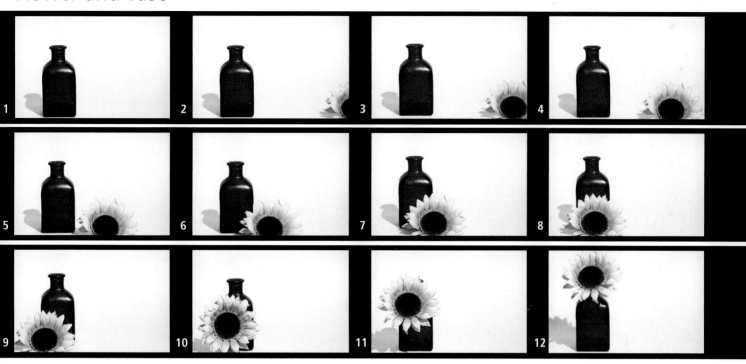

This sequence is a good demonstration of how effective very simple pixilation can be. The flower simply appears to the right of the frame and over 20 frames makes its way into the scene and up the side of the vase. The vase does not move. Even though the action is very simple, the flower does manage to convey a sense of character and performance.

# Anyone home?

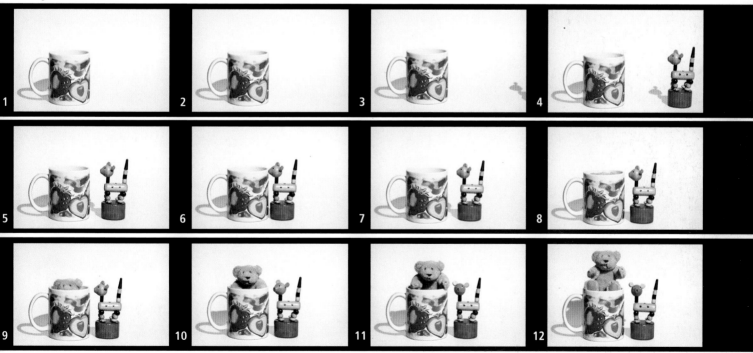

Sequences involving small toys can be enchanting. In this example, the wooden giraffe simply taps the side of the cup with his nose, and the bear pops up. When it comes to editing, this sequence makes for a challenging exercise, as you will need to time the taps to synchronize with the movement.

# 2D animation

Once you've grasped the basics of animating with a paper and pencil, you can easily create moving shapes and patterns and bring your drawings to life. A drawn sequence recorded under the camera (such as the growing flower below) is essentially a complex flip book. First the drawings are positioned on the copystand and framed under the camera. Then the computer records the images through the camera, stacks them in the correct order, and flips through them at a rate of 29.5 frames per second. Before you attempt the exercises on pages 66–67, there are two main issues you must understand and address: registration and aspect ratio.

## You will need

- sheets of letter paper
- field guide (see glossary, page 124)
- two-pin peg bar and hole punch
- tape
- pencil, sharpener, and eraser
- ruler
- felt-tip pens
- capure station setup for flat work (see page 18)
- lightbox (see page 28)

## Registration

In the context of drawn animation, registration is essentially making sure that the pages you are working on are bound together in some way to keep the images positioned correctly. When you are working under camera, you will need to bind your drawings together at two stages during production: 1) when drawing your images, and 2) when recording images under the camera. A device called a peg bar is used to bind the drawings.

**Peg bar**
The tool used in the animation industry to register drawings is called a "peg bar" (see above). A professional peg bar is a flat strip of plastic with three upright pegs. The peg on each end is flat, and the one in the middle is round. It works with paper that has been punched with holes that correspond to the three pegs on the bar. Although the punch used to make the holes in the paper for a professional peg bar is prohibitively expensive, there is an affordable option for the beginner. Chromacolour (a large international supplier of animation tools and equipment) sells a two-pin peg bar that has been designed to work with a standard two-hole paper punch. This is ideal for the beginner animator or an animator on a budget.

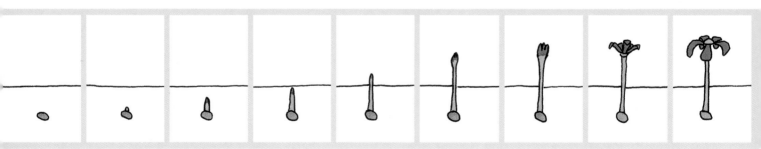

*In this sequence the ground does not change position, but the flower does. When you flip through these drawings, the flower appears to grow. The movement is achieved through accurate registration.*

# Aspect ratio

The second issue when producing drawn animation is an awareness of the size and shape of the captured image. Your camera will capture an image that is the same ratio as a standard television or computer screen. What makes this confusing is the fact that at the moment there are two standard sizes available as a setting on most cameras: 16:9 (the shape of a widescreen television or computer screen) and 4:3 (the standard shape for older television screens and computer monitors). Since playback screens made today are 16:9, the exercises in this book assume this aspect ratio. So, make sure your camera shoots in 16:9.

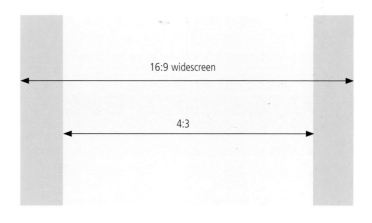

16:9 widescreen

4:3

# Peg bar and lightbox setup for shooting 2D animation

Always draw your images using this peg bar and lightbox combination. As long as your pages are on the peg bar on the lightbox when you draw them and are placed back on the peg bar on the lightbox when you shoot them, your drawings will always be perfectly registered. You can work with three or four sheets of paper at a time, and because you are working on a lightbox, you will clearly see the shape and position of the previous drawings, making it easier to decide where to place the next motif in the sequence. When you are ready to shoot the sequence, simply tape the peg bar down onto the surface and place the first drawing on it. Shoot the drawing, then take it off, and replace it with the next page in the sequence. Continue until you have shot each drawing on the peg bar.

1 Punch your sheets of paper and the field guide with a two-hole punch. Tape a two-pin peg bar onto the surface of a lightbox, and then place the field guide on the pegs.

2 Place a sheet of paper over the field guide and select the size you would like to work in. Carefully trace that rectangle onto the paper, using a ruler.

3 Remove both pages from the peg bar and put your field guide away for future use. Put the traced sheet with the rectangle back on the peg bar and place a new sheet of paper on top. You should clearly see the outline of the rectangle through the paper. You can now begin drawing your animation on this sheet, and continue by placing new sheets on top. Before you move onto the next image drawing, number the bottom right-hand corner of each page.

# Making it move: 2D

These exercises demonstrate a very simple approach to drawn animation, working with the peg bar and lightbox setup described on page 65.

## Expanding circle

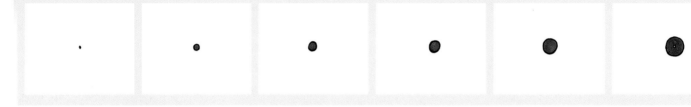

1 Using a pencil, draw a small circle in the center of the frame. Place another sheet of paper onto the peg bar and use felt-tip pens to draw another slightly bigger circle around the first.

2 Place another sheet of paper over the last and draw a slightly bigger circle around the first. Continue in the same way. When it becomes difficult to see through the paper, remove the bottom pages, but keep the traced field-size rectangle on the bar. Replace the last image you drew to use as a guide, then continue drawing.

3 When the circle gets big enough, begin another small circle in the center. Continue to add circles, and allow them to grow until they are outside the field-size rectangle. Use fifty sheets of paper.

## The yawn

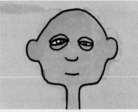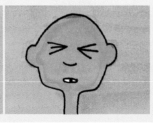

1 Draw a simple face using a pencil. Trace it three or four times without changing anything. When the sequence is shot, these images will create something called a "boil" (see step 5). Over the next 5 frames, close the eyes until they are squeezed shut.

2 Slowly, over the next 30 to 40 frames, make the mouth open wide by drawing a simple circle shape getting bigger and bigger. Add a new sheet of paper for each mouth shape, while always keeping the previous drawing on the peg bar. It is a good idea to keep the first drawing on the bar also, to avoid gradually losing the shape from page to page.

3 When the mouth is as wide as it can get, simply trace that drawing four times without changing anything. Continue drawing, but this time make the mouth smaller and smaller. Try to get it back to its original position in half the number of frames, because when you yawn your mouth opens slowly and closes quickly.

*Play the sequence back to check that the animation moves well. If you have a frame or two that look a little jerky, you can remove them from the animation, redraw them (correcting the mistake), and reshoot the sequence.*

4 When all the paper has been used, position the peg bar under the camera and place the traced field size on the pegs. Adjust the position of the camera and the paper until the rectangle is perfectly framed in the LCD screen and live-capture window. Secure the peg bar in position with tape.

5 Place one of the drawings on the bar (preferably one of the later drawings with lots of lines) and adjust the focus, white balance, and lighting until the image is evenly lit and sharp. Remove all the paper from the peg bar and place the first drawing only onto the pegs. Shoot a 50-frame hold.

6 Remove the first drawing, replace it with the second, and shoot 2 more frames. Repeat until you have shot the entire sequence. When you have completed and tested the basic drawings, introduce color using felt-tip pens or ink.

*Try using the technique below to make a sequence showing a chick hatching from an egg.*

    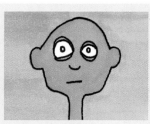

4 Trace the last drawing three or four times, but without changing anything at all.

5 You can shoot a hold by shooting the first image 30 times, but a difference in the quality of the line as soon as the action begins will be very noticeable. A little trick to keep your line lively during the hold is to shoot something called a "boil." To add a boil to a static image, simply trace the image four times. Then, shooting in 2s, shoot those frames in a random sequence until you have shot 30 frames. Then continue the sequence. The boil will lend an energetic, hand-drawn look to the hold, rather than a dead single frame that suddenly jumps into action with the first move.

6 Position and frame your work as you did for the previous exercise. Shoot in 2s and add a boil at the beginning and end of the action. Once you have shot the sequence and tested the line of your animation, you can ink over the lines in black pen and color the sequence in. You can even revisit the drawing, adding in teeth and a tongue if you like.

# 2D sequences in camera

2D animating is like putting a flip book under the camera. Whatever you can draw you can animate (and what you can't draw you can always trace, cut out, or collage). Use your imagination and be inspired by the themes below to create great animations filled with movement and energy.

## Taking a line for a walk

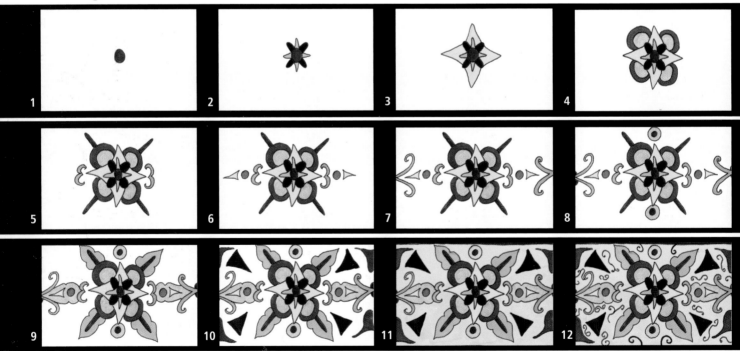

Rather than capturing a specific action, this sequence is made by simply building the drawing up, frame by frame, on one sheet of paper. This explorative technique is rather similar to sand animation and can be very attractive. Color is added with felt-tip pens.

# Bouncing figure

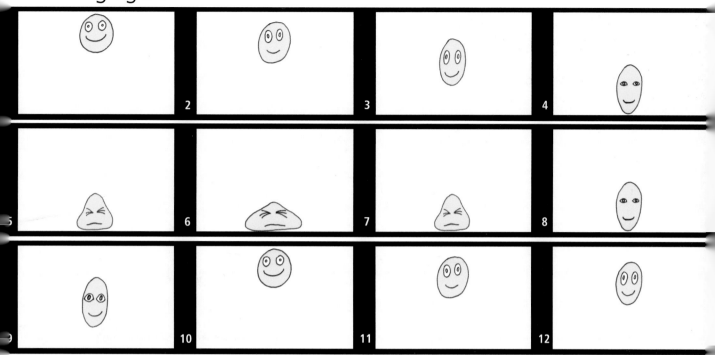

This sequence demonstrates a principle of animation known as squash and stretch. The figure appears wide and flat when it hits the ground and tall and thin when it springs upward.

# Snail into whale

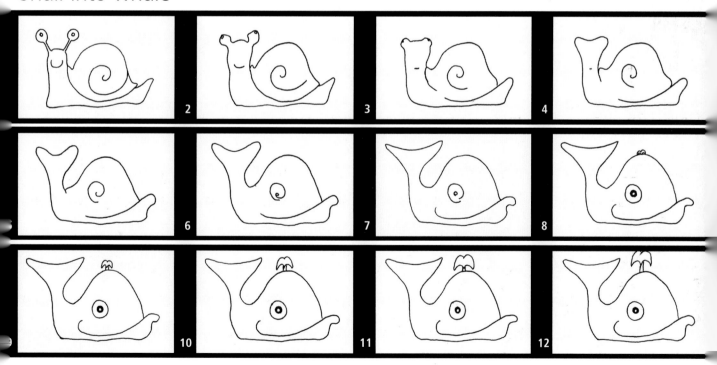

This sequence demonstrates a simple morphing cycle. The images were drawn in pencil, tested, and then inked over with a fine felt-tip pen to strengthen the line.

# Stop-motion **animation**

The term "stop-motion" refers to an animated sequence with characters that have been designed and built as free-standing three-dimensional objects. Stop-motion puppets can be made in a variety of ways and from many different materials, ranging from simple plasticine blobs to very complex silicone and metal characters used for stop-motion television programs and films. The puppet in this section is built around an aluminum wire and polymorph armature using foam, polymer clays, and fabric.

> **Project tools**
> - capture station setup for 3D work (see page 20)
> - all materials listed in the "puppetmaker's toolbox" (see opposite)

## Puppet anatomy

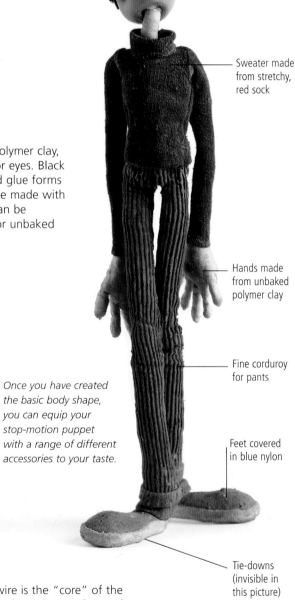

Black wool for hair

White glass beads for eyes

Head made from baked polymer clay

Sweater made from stretchy, red sock

Hands made from unbaked polymer clay

Fine corduroy for pants

Feet covered in blue nylon

Tie-downs (invisible in this picture)

*Once you have created the basic body shape, you can equip your stop-motion puppet with a range of different accessories to your taste.*

## Armature

An armature is essentially a flexible skeleton-like structure that will be rigid enough to support the finished puppet but flexible enough to allow it to move and bend. This armature is made from aluminum armature wire and a substance called "polymorph." The feet are part of the armature, but each one contains a nut and a screw that form a structure called a "tie-down." These tie-downs are vital when it comes to animating the character; they attach the puppet to the set and prevent it from falling over.

## Head

The head is made from polymer clay, with white glass beads for eyes. Black wool stiffened with wood glue forms the hair. The hands can be made with wire and foam, or they can be sculpted from plasticine or unbaked polymer clay.

Core

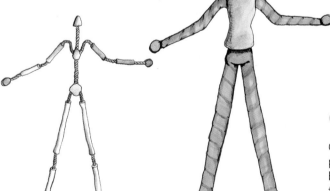

Armature

## Core

On top of the wire is the "core" of the puppet. Polymorph sections make up the bones, and the foam, which is light and flexible, forms the shape of the body. The core is then simply covered with fabric, which is stitched or glued in place.

# The puppetmaker's toolbox

## ALUMINUM ARMATURE WIRE

This wire will be twisted together to form the arms, legs, and spine of your puppet. Buy two types of wire: a 1.5mm and a 2 mm width (or gauge) aluminum wire. You can't prevent your wire from snapping eventually, but for the best results you can extend the life of your armature by twisting several strands of wire together. Later, you can design armatures that are easily repaired. At the outset, the beginner should build three or four identical replacement puppets.

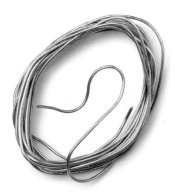

*With care you can shoot one minute's worth of animation with your armature.*

## POLYMORPH

This substance is found in the form of plastic strips or round balls. It becomes soft and pliable when dropped into hot water and remains soft for two to three minutes. As it cools, it hardens to form a strong, lightweight material. It is ideal for the first-time puppetmaker because it is easy to use, lightweight, and reusable. If you get it wrong the first time, simply dunk the part you are working on back into hot water, remelt the plastic, and try again.

*A strip of polymorph can be molded into shape after dipping it in hot water.*

*Don't use plastic beads, because they will melt in the oven when you bake the head.*

## BEADS

The easy way to create eyes is to make two holes with a pencil, but glass beads can give puppets cartoonish expressions. The best eyes are made from pressed glass beads. They are cheap, have a hole through them, and come in a range of sizes from ¼ in. (6mm) to ⅜ in. (10mm) wide. Later, you can learn to move the eyes with a pin while animating (for an eye-rolling effect).

*Foam used for making seat cushions is ideal for for padding the puppet's body.*

## FOAM

The ideal foam for puppetmaking is white, dense, very soft, and in sheets about ½ in. (1.5 cm) thick. A useful source is the backing from an ironing-board cover. Thin sheets are easiest to work with, but you can also slice thin strips from a large block with a craft knife.

## FABRICS

The best type of fabric for making clothes for puppets is any fine material with two-way stretch (manmade fabrics such as nylon are ideal). You may also need a needle and thread.

*Keep a rag bag of old socks, T-shirts, and pantyhose (brightly colored, if possible).*

## SCISSORS, SMALL WIRE CUTTERS, PLIERS

Armature building is a complex business, requiring lots of twisting, cutting, and bending. You'll need pliers and a sharp pair of scissors with a pointed end.

## OLIVE OIL OR BABY OIL

You will need this for the blink sequence on pages 90–93.

## GLUES

A hot-melt glue gun is essential for tie-downs. Hair can be stiffened and stuck to a polymer-clay head with wood glue. A latex-based glue is needed to make the puppet's foam-based core. It's also best to invest in a tube of epoxy glue.

*A hot-melt glue gun is required for tie-downs*

## HAND DRILL AND PICTURE HOOK

If you clamp the hook into the chuck of the drill, you can twist several strands of wire evenly together. This is vitally important when making a wire armature.

## NUTS, BOLTS, WING NUTS, SCREWS

These are essential when making tie-downs. Make several sets of tie-downs per puppet.

# Making a puppet armature

A few rough sketches of your character are essential when designing an armature, as the type of character will inform the size and position of the arms, legs, chest, etc. The stages of making the puppet include building an armature and padding it out, making clothes, and molding an expressive face and head. Take your time through the whole process—it can be challenging and requires some patience.

## The wire armature

### MAKING THE SPINE AND LEGS

1 Place a picture hook into the chuck of a drill and tighten. Using wire cutters, cut three 3 ft. (1 m) lengths of 2 mm gauge wire. Loop one end of each length around the picture hook and the other end around a fixed object (i.e. a door handle).

2 Pull the wire fairly taut and run the drill on a slow speed. The wire should begin to twist together evenly. Continue until the wire breaks. (This will always occur at one end or the other.) Repeat this step with two more strands of the same wire to form a shorter section of about 1 ft. (30 cm). The triple strand will be used for the spine of your puppet and the double strand for the legs.

3 Bend the double strand exactly in the middle to form a V-shape. This shape will form your puppet's legs. Take the triple twist of wire (the spine) and splay out the individual strands to about ¾–1¼ in. (2–3 cm) long using a pair of pliers. These short strands will help you to join the spine to the pelvis.

8 As soon as it is cool enough to work with, squeeze it into a sausage shape, then roll it into a fairly thin coil.

9 Trim 1¼–1½ in. (3–4 cm) of the polymorph and leave on the side for reuse.

10 Working as quickly as possible, take one end of the coil and press it firmly into the knot of wire made in step 4.

11 Now bring the polymorph strand up between the legs and wrap it snugly around the knot, pressing it firmly into the wire. Continue to wrap the knot, encasing the wire strands in the soft polymorph.

 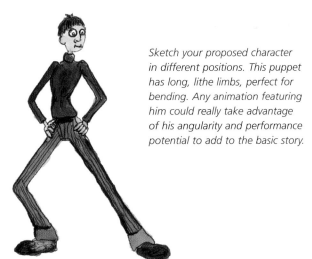

*Sketch your proposed character in different positions. This puppet has long, lithe limbs, perfect for bending. Any animation featuring him could really take advantage of his angularity and performance potential to add to the basic story.*

4 Wrap the splayed strands around the bend in the leg wire.

5 Trim off any loose ends with wire cutters and squeeze the section with pliers to tighten the joint as much as possible.

6 It is safer to follow the next steps in the kitchen. Boil water and pour it in a mug. Drop a small handful of polymorph beads into the cup and wait for about thirty to forty seconds.

7 Fish the melted material from the mug using the top of your scissors (never your fingers), and allow to cool slightly. You will see that the beads have fused together and the material has become slightly transparent. It now has the consistency of chewing gum, and is fairly hot to the touch.

 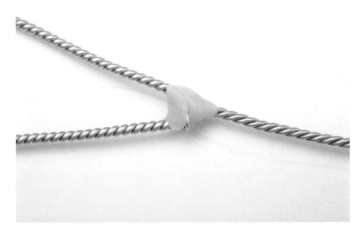

12 When the knot is completely covered, trim off any remaining polymorph and squeeze the whole section firmly for about sixty seconds, keeping your hand as still as possible.

13 The polymorph should begin to cool, and the joint should firm up. If there is any loose rattle in this section after the polymorph has cooled, simply dip the whole thing back into hot water, melt the polymorph off, and try again.

## Making the shoulders and arms

1 Make a ¾–1¼ in. (2–3 cm) gap in the spine by twisting the strands of wire open. You can do this with your fingers, or with pliers, but be gentle if you are using pliers because damaged wire will create a weak point. This gap will form the joint between the arm wire and the spine.

2 It is important to note that this joint does not mark the shoulder line on the puppet. The wire bends upward from this point to shoulder height, then curves downward again to form the arms. This design allows the puppet to move his shoulders forward and backward, which is important for his performance.

3 Twist two to three strands of 16 in. (40 cm) lengths of 1.5 mm wire together using the drill, as before. Thread one end through the gap in the spine, and pull through the piece to a little over halfway. This will form the shoulders and arms.

4 Wrap the longer end of the arm wire tightly around the thicker spine wire.

## Making the bones

You've now created an armature with a flexible set of limbs. If you were to animate the puppet at this stage however, the arms and legs would move like spaghetti, because you haven't yet created any rigid "bones" for your character. You can now make these rigid sections by wrapping parts of the wire in thin strips of polymorph.

*You will need to make two bones for each leg and two for each arm. The upper leg is a little longer than the lower leg, and the upper arm is longer than the lower arm. Each section of "bone" should be just wide enough to wrap around the wire when it is soft. Spend some time drawing the length and location of each bone rectangle in pencil first, because the positioning of these sections will dictate the proportions of your finished puppet.*

1 Melt a handful of polymorph in hot water and pinch it flat between your fingers. Make it more even by rolling it out with a bottle or a rolling pin.

2 Using a pair of scissors, trim the rolled polymorph into a rectangle. You are aiming to make a shape that will just about wrap around the wire and will be long enough to form the rigid part of the upper leg.

3 Starting with the upper leg, soften the polymorph strip by dipping it in boiling water using the tip of the scissors. Working quickly and referring to your bone drawing, position the strip against the upper leg section of your armature.

4 Working from back to front, pinch the soft polymorph around the wire.

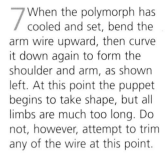

**7** When the polymorph has cooled and set, bend the arm wire upward, then curve it down again to form the shoulder and arm, as shown left. At this point the puppet begins to take shape, but all limbs are much too long. Do not, however, attempt to trim any of the wire at this point.

**5** Melt another small amount of polymorph (or remelt what was left over from joining the legs and spine) and wrap the new wire joint as tightly as you can. Try to use as little polymorph as possible in order to form a small, neat joint.

**6** Squeeze the cooling polymorph tightly to keep the wire tight and prevent it from wobbling about and opening up the joint.

*Shoulders and arms play a big part in conveying character. Throwing the shoulders back creates a much different impression than when they are slumped forward.*

**5** When the polymorph comes into contact with itself it should stick together quite easily. If it will not stick, it has cooled down too much. In this case, dip the whole leg into hot water and pull off the softened polymorph. You can do this as often as you like: It may take many attempts before your rigid polymorph bone is firmly in place in the correct location.

**6** Continue adding each polymorph bone section in the same way until you have upper and lower legs and upper and lower arms.

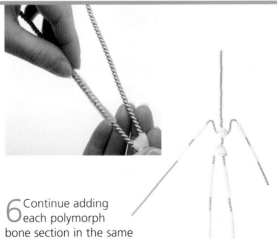

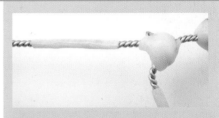

**TIP**
When positioning the bones, you will need to leave a fairly large gap between the polymorph sections. These gaps essentially become the puppet's joints, and your puppet will move better and last longer if there is plenty of space between the bones.

## MAKING FEET AND TIE-DOWNS

The puppet's feet incorporate a tie-down system: They are built with a hole running through them, which is lined up with a corresponding hole drilled into the tabletop. From underneath, a threaded screw is pushed up through the tabletop and screwed into the puppet's foot, securing the character to the surface. Follow these simple instructions to make your own set of tie-downs on your armature.

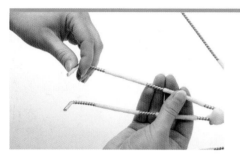

1 Bend the leg wire forward to form the foot. Make sure you leave at least ¾ in. (2 cm) of wire to form the ankle joint. Trim the extra wire, leaving a 1¼ in. (3 cm) section.

2 Using a pair of pliers, gently splay out the wire in the foot, taking care not to damage it by squeezing too hard. With the tip of the pliers, curl the wire on the inside of the leg into a spiral, and curl the wire on the outside of the leg around this inner spiral.

3 Take two screws with hexagonal nuts ⅛ in. (3mm) wide and 1¼ in. (3 cm) long. Screw the nut through the bolt to about two-thirds of the length of the screw. Fit the screw into the inside spiral of the foot, with the head of the screw under the foot and the bolt resting flat on top of the wire spiral. Secure the nut and bolt in this position with gun glue.

7 Fit the slit in the polymorph disk around the screw and press it together so that the screw is poking out of the top of the polymorph disk.

8 This polymorph disk will become your puppet's foot. Mold the polymorph into the shape of a foot with a flat base, dipping it back into the mug from time to time to keep the polymorph workable and soft.

9 The screw should remain sticking out of the top and bottom of the foot, and the nut should remain firmly stuck to the wire inside the polymorph. If at any point the screw and nut become loose and wobble inside the polymorph, simply dip the foot into hot water, peel the polymorph off when it softens, and start again. It may take a few attempts to get this stage right, but it is worth the effort, because rock-solid tie-downs will make you a more confident animator.

**Measure your proportions**

*Take a look at your own arm. With a ruler, measure the distance between the crook of your elbow and the middle of your wrist. Now measure the distance between the middle of your wrist and the tip of your longest finger. This distance will vary from person to person, but most of us are surprised at how long the hand actually is.*

4 Pour some freshly boiled water into a mug and melt a small amount of polymorph. Roll this into a ball. Pinch the ball between your fingers to flatten it slightly, forming a disk shape.

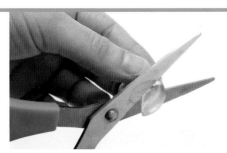

5 Use scissors to cut through from the edge to the center of the disk.

6 Soften the polymorph again by dipping it into boiled water for thirty seconds, then bring it to the top of the puppet's foot.

## MAKING ARMS AND HANDS

It can be difficult to get the proportions of your character right the first time you build a puppet. This is especially true when it comes to arm length and hand positions. Typically, the first-time puppetmaker must make a decision about the positioning of the puppet's elbows and wrists and underestimate how long the hands will be. The result is a puppet whose fingertips are lower than its knees.

1 By now your puppet should resemble something human shaped. Using the existing proportions of shoulder height, etc., make a decision as to the position of the puppet's hands, and cut the arm wire at the spot where you imagine the palms of the hands would be.

2 As with the foot, splay the ends of the wire out slightly with a pair of pliers, and curl them to form a small loop at the end of the arm.

3 Using your glue gun, carefully squeeze a small amount of glue onto the wire loop. The glue may drip through the wire, so make sure you work over a table and that your hands are clear of any hot drips. When the glue has cooled a little, wet your fingers and carefully pinch it into a small disk shape. The aim here is to cover the wire and to create a solid circle of glue at the end of each arm. You can add more glue if necessary, but try to keep these pads as small as possible. You will finish the hands off in the next section, "Adding body and shape."

MAKING THE NECK

1 Make a decision on the length of the neck based on the proportions of the armature as a whole. In the final puppet, the end of the neck wire will be located about halfway up inside the character's head. Trim the neck wire to the correct length with your pliers.

2 As before, splay out the ends of the wire a little.

3 Melt a small amount of polymorph and shape it between your fingers to form a rough cone shape, wider at one end. With the polymorph as hot as possible, push the cone shape down over the splayed wires.

4 As you push it down over the wire the polymorph may lose its shape, but you can easily dip it back into hot water and shape it into a neat cone again using your fingers. With a tool edge, tidy up the base of the cone, making it as neat as possible.

# Adding body and shape

The next stage is to add bulk to the puppet. This process is sometimes referred to as "skinning" the puppet. A simple, inexpensive approach for beginners is the "build up" method. Here, materials such as upholstery foam and fabric are used to make a lightweight and flexible body.

Note the position of the tie-down screw. It is much easier to screw it in and out if you add a wingnut (see page 89 for details).

Thin strips of foam and a latex-based glue.

## COVERING THE LEGS

1 Paint a layer of latex-based glue on one leg of your armature, from the foot up to the puppet's waist.

2 Take a thin foam sheet and cut a strip ½–¾ in. (1½–2 cm) wide and about 16 in. (40 cm) long. Paint a thick layer of glue on one side of the strip and squeeze it in your hand to soak the entire length of the strip in the glue. Allow the glue to go tacky (about five minutes). Beginning at the top of the leg, wrap the strip tightly around the armature, keeping the edges neat.

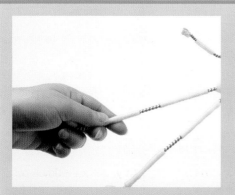

## The rattle test

The entire armature, when you have added core material to your whole puppet (see pages 80–81), should behave as if it were made from a single piece of wire.

To ensure that you have achieved this goal, take your puppet by one foot and shake it rapidly up and down. If any part of the armature rattles or appears loose, your puppet has failed the test and you need to resolve the issue before you move on. Any loose part, whether it be a joint or a polymorph bone that is not quite tight, will tend to shimmy about while you are animating. This movement will appear in a final sequence as a sort of low-voltage wiggle that will distract attention from your puppet's performance, and from the story you are telling.

3 Continue wrapping the leg until you have reached the foot. Cover half the foot in the strip, then trim it neatly with scissors. Repeat the same steps for the other leg and the arms, moving from the shoulder to just beyond the wrist before trimming the strip.

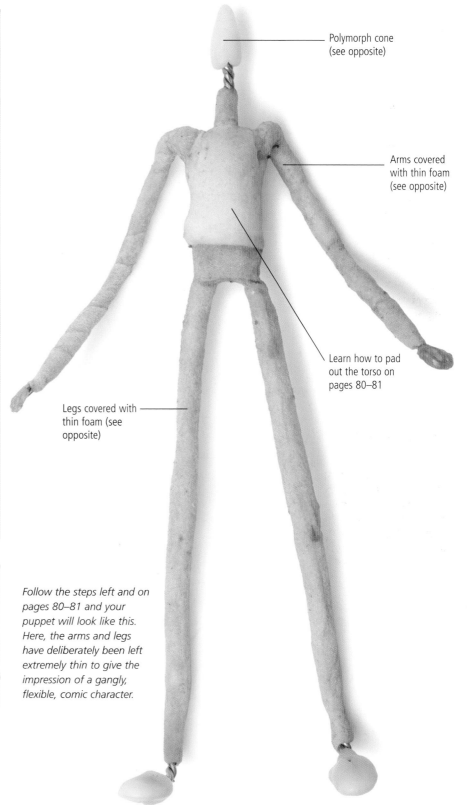

Polymorph cone
(see opposite)

Arms covered
with thin foam
(see opposite)

Learn how to pad
out the torso on
pages 80–81

Legs covered with
thin foam (see
opposite)

*Follow the steps left and on pages 80–81 and your puppet will look like this. Here, the arms and legs have deliberately been left extremely thin to give the impression of a gangly, flexible, comic character.*

## COVERING THE FEET

  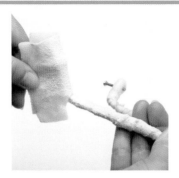 

1 Using a very thin foam sheet, cut a square about ⁵⁄₁₆ x ⁵⁄₁₆ in. (8 x 8mm), and trim out a small U shape halfway down one side. Soak this in latex-based glue.

2 Slot the puppet's leg into the U shape, and press gently on the top of the foot to stick the foam to the polymorph.

3 Pull the foam firmly down over the foot so that it begins to take the shape of the polymorph underneath.

4 Trim the edges behind the foot, and tuck any excess foam inward, pinching it to stick the hem down.

## PADDING OUT THE TORSO

1 To make the body of the puppet you will need to use a thicker sheet of foam, at least ¾ in. (2 cm) thick. Cut the foam into a rectangle shape that will cover the puppet from shoulders to waistline. This section will wrap around the puppet, forming the torso. Cut two slits along one side to fit underneath the arms.

2 Paint a thick layer of latex-based glue on both sides of the foam. Encourage the glue to soak through by squeezing the foam in your fist. This is messy but ensures that the glue has saturated every bit of the foam. Allow the glue to dry for five minutes. The foam will become very adhesive, sticking easily to itself and to the armature. Begin to fit the foam to the torso by attaching it to the front of the armature. You can easily trim the foam square down if you feel that the shape needs to be modified for a better fit.

3 Pull the foam around to the back of the puppet, fitting the arms into the slits. If there is excess foam, simply trim it to fit.

4 Pinch the edges of the foam together at the back of the puppet to form a neat seam. If the edges don't stick, add more glue along each edge.

5 Using your finger and thumb, pinch the edges together, forming a neat seam running down the puppet's heel. Gather the loose foam at the front and pull downward, pinching it all together under the foot. You may find it useful to remove the tie-down at this point. Leave the puppet to dry for about twenty minutes.

6 With sharp scissors, trim the excess foam away, working as close to the base of the foot as possible. Make sure that the tie-down hole is clear of foam and glue. Repeat the same steps for the other foot and replace the tie-downs.

**Shaping your characters**

*If your character is tall and thin, one layer of foam will be enough on the limbs. However, if you wish to pad out any area, (thicker arms for a weightlifter character, for example) simply add another strip to that section.*

5 Close the shoulder seams along the top of the torso in the same way. For a neater finish, fold the raw edges back and in slightly to form a hem on each edge before you stick them together.

6 With your thumbs and forefingers, pinch the foam around the shoulders and arms into shape and hold for about thirty seconds. If the glue has not dried out too much, the foam will begin to hold its shape, allowing you to sculpt a little by nipping in the waist and rounding the shoulders.

7 Cut a thin strip of the same foam sheet used to bulk out the arms and legs, and paint it with glue. Wrap it around the neck wire once or twice to make a thicker neck.

8 Paint the entire torso with a thin layer of glue to help reinforce all the seams. Your skinned armature should look like the puppet on page 79. Note the color change as the glue dries out. The final result should be a light, flexible puppet.

# Making the costume and head

When choosing a fabric for your puppet's costume, remember that the best type is thin and, if possible, stretchy. If the fabric is too thick the puppet looks less convincing, and the costume's bulk will inhibit movement. A plain colored fabric or fabrics with a very simple, small-scale pattern will be less distracting than highly patterned fabric. Choose a material that is tightly woven since loosely woven fabric can fray at the edges, making it difficult to sew and causing loose threads.

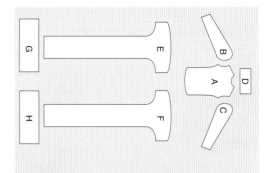

## FREE STUFF

On page 122 you will find a basic pattern (like the smaller one above) for the puppet's sweater and pants. Either clothes can be glued in place or sewn together directly onto the puppet. Gluing the fabric is a quicker process but it can be messy, and the finish is never as neat as a sewn costume. Sewing is always the better option, but it is a time-consuming process and difficult if you don't have a lot of experience with a needle and thread. The steps demonstrate both processes, with the puppet's pants glued in place and the sweater hand stitched.

## The costume

### MAKING THE PUPPET'S FOOTWEAR

To cover the feet, you need a material that is very flexible and stretchy. Use either thick nylon pantyhose or very fine socks. Pantyhose are recommended because they have a shiny finish, which looks much more like shoe leather than soft woolly fabric.

1 Paint the entire foam surface of the foot in glue and cover with a square of fabric. Stretch the fabric downward and hold in position for a minute or so, until it sticks to the foam.

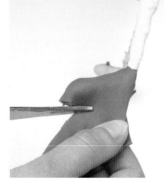

2 When the fabric has adhered to the foam, trim the excess away with sharp scissors, keeping the tension in the fabric with your hand and running the blade close to the base of the foot.

3 Paint glue onto the loose edges of the trimmed fabric, taking care to keep the top of the shoe clean. When the glue grows tacky, fold these edges in and press into the sole of the foot with your finger.

4 From the thin foam sheet, cut a rough foot shape a little larger than the puppet's own foot, and soak with glue. Cut a hole to allow for the tie-down.

1 On the back of the fabric, draw out a tapered rectangle a little longer than the distance between the puppet's waistline and foot. Cut the shape out with sharp scissors. This will be a pant leg and will fit snugly to the upper leg and waist after it has been hemmed. Fit the fabric to the puppet's leg and trim if necessary.

2 Using a fine paintbrush, paint a thin layer of latex-based glue around the edges of the fabric, taking care not to smear any on the front of the material. Allow the glue to dry a little, for about five to ten minutes.

3 When the glue is tacky, carefully fold a narrow seam over, pressing firmly to stick the fabric onto itself. Continue until there is a seam all around the material.

4 Repeat steps 1 to 3 to make the second leg of the pants, fitting the sections to the puppet to work out the necessary length and width. The sections for the sweater are made in the same way, but cut from the red cloth.

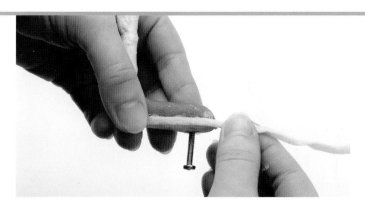

5 Allow a few minutes for the glue to become tacky and press the shape firmly to the base of the foot. Allow a few minutes to dry out, then trim with sharp scissors to the contours of the foot.

6 Adding a trim to the edge of the shoe looks good and tidies up the joint between the fabric and the sponge. Simply cut a very thin strip of the foam sheet, soak it in glue, and run it around the bottom of the shoe.

7 To neaten up the joint even further, you can glue a small folded piece of fabric into place to form a turned-up pant cuff.

1 Carefully paint a thin layer of latex-based glue onto the back of one pant leg, and then fit the section to the front of the leg, making sure it is in the correct position.

2 Using a fine paintbrush, dab a small amount of glue along the length of each seam, and allow the glue to dry out a little.

3 Glue the open ends of the pants to the lower half of the torso. Working your way down the length of the leg, press and pinch the edges together between finger and thumb to close the seam neatly. When adding the second leg, allow the top sections to overlap front and back to create the top of the pants.

4 Fit the front and back of the sweater to the puppet's torso, securing them in place with a small dab of glue if necessary.

# The head

A simple and expressive head can be easily made using polymer clay. Use the puppet's body to gauge the size of the head.

## MAKING THE HEAD

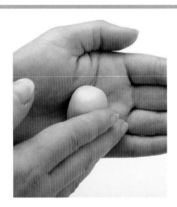

*You will need a ball of polymer clay to make your puppet's head.*

1 Work the ball of polymer clay between your fingers to warm and soften it. This is known as "conditioning" the clay and is an important step, because badly conditioned clay can remain stiff and difficult to shape. When it is fully softened and mixed, roll an even oval/egg shape in the clay.

2 To make the puppet's nose form a small cone shape and flatten one side. Roll a small ball, flatten it, and slice it in half for his ears.

3 Position the nose and ears on the head and press lightly to join the clay. Using your fingers, smooth over the joins to blend. Tidy up the face with a moist baby wipe. This is a tricky process and you may need two attempts before you are satisfied.

5 Adjust the seams so they match up perfectly. Using red sewing thread and a thimble, join both halves together by sewing a neat seam from the bottom of the sweater up to the puppet's arm. Turn the puppet over and repeat the same process on the other side. Close the shoulder seams on the top in the same manner.

6 Fit the sleeve section with the seam positioned along the bottom of the arm. Pinch the seams together with your fingers and thumb, and neatly sew the seam shut working from the wrist to the armpit of the puppet. Using the smallest, neatest stitches possible, sew around the top of the arm, attaching the sleeve to the main body of the sweater.

7 The easiest way to finish the puppet's costume is by adding a turtleneck collar to the sweater and turned up cuffs to the bottom of the pants. This is very simply done by cutting a thin strip of the fabric, making a thick hem on both edges, and trimming it to fit around the puppet's neck. It can then be glued or stitched in place.

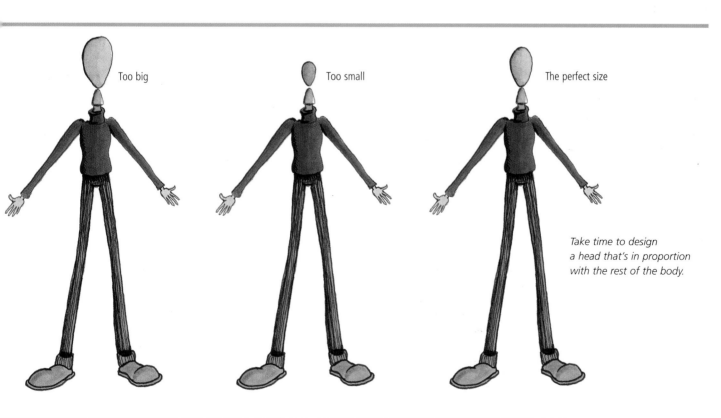

Too big

Too small

The perfect size

*Take time to design a head that's in proportion with the rest of the body.*

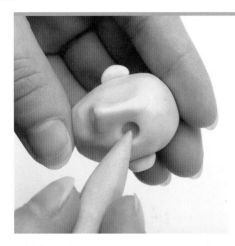

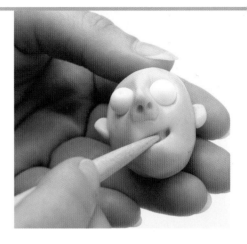

4 Using a pencil or modeling tool, gently push the tip into the base of the nose, creating two nostrils. You will also need to make two shallow sockets for the eyes. These holes should be slightly less than half the bead in depth.

5 Gently press the bead into the eye socket, sinking half of it into the clay and leaving the other half above the surface. If you are careful at this stage you can create an eye that can be moved when the head has been baked. Repeat this step with the second bead.

6 Using a pencil or modeling tool, press gently into the clay to form an open mouth shape. With your finger and thumb on either side of the mouth, pinch the face in gently.

## MAKING THE HAIR

1 To make the hair, simply wrap the black yarn several times around the fingers of one hand.

2 Slip the whole thing off your hand and tie tightly in the middle with a piece of the same wool.

3 Trim the looped edges with a scissors to form a loose fringe all the way around. Paint each strand with a thin layer of wood glue, working it between your fingers so that all of the strands are soaked with glue.

7 Gently press the chin up to close the mouth. This should form a nice smiling shape.

8 With a side-to-side twisting motion, ease the head down onto the polymorph cone at the neck top. Stop when you feel the head is in the correct position in relation to the shoulders (the neck cone should be completely covered and the head straight). Ease the head off the neck and bake.

*Take care at this stage because it is easy to put too much pressure on the clay, causing the head to squash and distort. A gentle hand is required at all times when handling unbaked polymer clay. When the head has been baked and fully cooled down, you can add the finishing touches.*

### Making the eyes
Use two white glass beads for the eyes. These must be glass, because plastic or resin beads will melt in the oven. Here we have used 5/16 in. (8mm) "pressed glass beads," but you can use any size, from 1/4 to 1/2 in. (6 to 12mm), depending on the size of your puppet's head.

*In some cases the beads can be moved around with a pin, and the puppet can move its eyes. However, it can be difficult to get right every time, because the beads will sometimes stick to the clay. The trick is knowing how far to push the bead while the clay is still soft, a skill that comes with practice.*

4 Attach the hair to the puppet's head and smooth each strand into place with your fingers. Leave overnight for the wood glue to set. When it has fully set, the hair should be stiff and firmly glued to the head.

5 With a sharp scissors, trim the hair into the desired shape.

*A spot of black nail polish for the pupil of the eye will last permanently.*

1 If you push the head back down over the polymorph cone, you run the risk of cracking the head since the polymer clay can shrink when baked. First soften the polymorph cone on the neck by dipping it in hot water. It will then slip easily into the hole in the head. Work the head from side to side to refit it on the neck. Then remove the head again and allow the polymorph to cool.

2 To glue the head to the body use a very strong glue. Try a two-part epoxy glue with a very strong bond. Mix the parts following the manufacturer's instructions.

3 Smear the glue generously onto the polymorph cone at the top of the neck.

4 Work the head back down over the polymorph and glue using a gentle side-to-side motion.

# Finishing touches: making replacement hands

You can make the hands in the same way as you made the body: by covering a wire armature with strips of foam and glue. But it is a difficult process that requires a degree of skill and experience. So, for your first puppet, make hands from modeling clay or unbaked polymer clay. This type of hand is very flexible and animates well, but it is easily and quickly damaged. Because of this, the hands should be the last thing you attach to your puppet. Make up to five or six pairs of identical hands and keep them to one side when animating. Then, when a hand becomes squashed during shooting, pull it off and attach a new one.

1 Roll a small ball of clay between your finger and thumb and pinch it flat. This will form your puppet's palm.

2 Roll a series of sausage shapes and gently press them into place on the palm. These will form the fingers.

3 Add a shorter thumb shape. Then use the tip of your finger to gently smooth the soft clay thumb over the joined sections.

4 Using a scalpel or modeling tool, carefully make a small slit in the base of the palm.

# Tie-downs and tabletops

You might remember that you built the foot around a nut and a screw, and that the nut is lodged firmly inside each foot. This nut forms one half of your tie-down system, and the screw forms the other half. The puppet's feet are placed over holes drilled into the set, and the screws are threaded up through the holes and screwed into place inside the puppet's foot to attach him firmly to the table. A wing nut, glued onto the base of each screw, helps you to twist it into place.

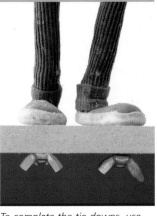

To complete the tie-downs, use two ⅛ in. (3mm) screws, two ⅛ in. (3mm) nuts, and two wing nuts that fit the screws. The epoxy glue dries clear and isn't visible in this photograph.

1 For teaching purposes, this sequence shows the workings of the nut and screw demonstrated independently of the foot. Thread the wing nut onto the screw, then add the nut.

2 Screw the nut all the way down the shaft of the screw until it reaches the wing nut. Tighten the nut using a pair of pliers and paint a thick layer of epoxy glue all around the end of the tie-down, encasing the tightened bolt. Allow to dry overnight. It is a good idea to make up a few spare tie-downs, because occasionally the wing nut works its way loose from the glue. Keep them screwed into the puppet's feet when not in use to avoid losing them.

5 Wipe off any excess glue with a tissue. Make sure the head is straight and in the correct position, and leave to dry overnight.

5 Gently ease the hand down over the disk at the end of the puppet's arm until it reaches the sleeve's edge.

6 Tidy up the hand and make sure that the armature is covered all the way around.

## TIP

In order to secure the puppet to the table using the tie-downs, you'll need to drill some holes. Find an old, unwanted table that you can drill holes into, or if drilling is not an option, clamp a square of particle board to an existing table, protecting the table beneath with folded fabric. Allow the particle board to overhang the surface by 6–8 in. (15–20 cm) and use that area for your drilled holes.

# Making it move: stop-motion animation

Once your puppet is fixed to the surface and your camera and lights are set up, you can test out your puppet. You will find that it is very easy to produce some kind of motion initially, because any change to the puppet's position between frames will make the character move. Indeed you will probably have the puppet flapping its arms and twitching its fingers in a matter of minutes. What is more difficult is to produce a believable, subtle performance. In order to understand the way a character might move or react, it is a good idea to act out the story yourself and analyze your body language and expressions. You may feel a little foolish, but your puppet's performance will be ten times better.

## Blink sequence

Act out the following three scenarios in front of a mirror and use your facial expressions only.

• You are quietly reading a book and suddenly shocked by a loud noise behind you.
• You have just left the house, and you get a nagging feeling that you may have forgotten something important.
• You have just done something wrong, and you are trying to charm your way out of trouble.

Did you use a blink to emphasize any of these mini performances? It may seem like a tiny, insignificant detail, but blinking is an important acting tool for your puppet. It brings your puppet to life and helps him or her to correctly register facial expressions.

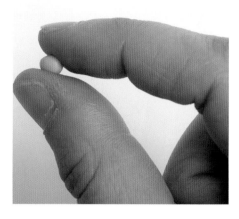

1 Roll a tiny ball of polymer clay between your finger and thumb. When pinched flat, this ball should cover the entire eye bead. If it is too large, use a smaller piece.

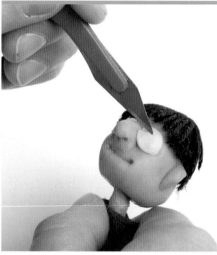

5 Using a craft knife, gently cut a line along one eye, making a thin crescent shape close to the top of the lid.

2 When you have found the correct size make up five or six identical lid shapes. These shapes will be trimmed to form a series of replacement lids.

3 Using a paintbrush, dab a very small amount of oil onto the puppet's eye. This should prevent the clay from sticking to the bead too much.

4 Place the first pair of lids over both eyes and gently ease them over the visible part of the beads. Don't worry if it looks a little crude, as these shapes will only be on screen for a couple of frames.

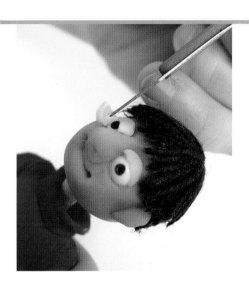

6 With the tip of the blade, gently peel the lower section of one lid away from the eye, taking great care not to nudge the puppet out of position. Repeat the last two steps on the other eye, making a matching pair of lids.

7 Position the head so that it is looking slightly to the right of the frame.

8 Shooting in twos, gradually move its head so that it is now completely in profile and looking right.

9 Using the tip of the craft knife, gently peel the first set of lids away. Cover both eyes with another full lid, and again, cut a line across each lid from left to right. This time, however, cut a straight line halfway down the eyeball. Peel away the bottom half of the lids with the tip of the knife. Now the eyes should appear half closed.

10 Shoot 2 frames. Remove the half-closed lids and cover the entire eye with another polymer clay disk. Shoot 2 more frames.

11 To open the eyes again, simply repeat the previous steps in reverse, going from the fully closed shape (step 4) to the half closed shape (step 6) to almost open (Step 10) to fully open, as shown above.

# Wave sequence

While watching the action in a mirror, hold your left hand up, with the fingers wide and the palm facing out. Keeping your fingers and wrist as stiff as you can, move your hand and lower arm rapidly from side to side about ten times by flexing at the elbow only. Now, close your eyes and imagine you are at a party and you have just glanced up to see a very good friend across the room. Open your eyes and wave to your reflection as if it were that friend.

You should notice a real difference between both actions. The first wave looks and feels stiff and forced, while the second wave is much more relaxed and natural. This is because the second time you waved you didn't have to think about the movement, and you reacted as if you were trying to attract the attention of that friend of yours. The elbow barely moved, and all the action came from the wrist. The fingers will also have been more relaxed.

## CREATING A WAVE SEQUENCE

1 Framing the puppet from the knees up, pose him so that his arms are down by his sides and his head is turned to the left. Shoot a 30-frame hold. Over 15 frames, turn the head so that it is facing the camera, and add in a blink by following the previous exercise.

2 You are now going to bring the arm and the hand into the correct position for the wave. Gradually bring the lower arm up to the correct height by flexing it at the elbow a little, shooting 2 frames, flexing it again, shooting 2 more etc., until you have shot 7 or so frames and the arm is in the correct position to wave.

12 When you play this sequence back the puppet should perform a simple blink. To slow the blink down, add more lid shapes (five instead of three); to speed it up, use just two shapes. It may take a few attempts to master the blink exercise, but it is well worth perfecting. When you become confident with the basic process, try a few different combinations of head movements and blinking sequences.

3 While the arm moves upward the wrist remains limp and the hand and fingers remain in a relaxed hanging position.

4 When the arm reaches the correct position, shoot a 5-frame hold, then over the next 5 or so frames move the hand and fingers from this relaxed position into an upright pose, and spread the fingers out to prepare the hand for the wave. Shoot a 5-frame hold.

5 The actual wave movement is created by bending the wrist joint only. The hand will move five times to travel from one side of the wave action to the other. On frame 6, it will change course and begin to move in the other direction. Note how the puppet's fingers have been bent slightly back against the direction the hand is traveling in. This trick helps the movement to appear more lively and real and is a basic demonstration of a fundamental animation principal known as "drag."

# Acting and performance

You can greatly enhance your puppet's performance by identifying not just what the character is doing but what he is thinking while he is doing it.

## Simple bow

The first bow tends to involve a simple dipping of the head, sometimes with one palm briefly held to the stomach. It is often stiff and is usually very fast.

1 Knees flexed, arms at his sides, eyes forward, the puppet gets ready for his bow.

2 Use the blink technique to drop his eyelids as if he is modest. His shoulders slump further.

3 The puppet now seems to curl forward at the waist.

4 Suddenly his knees straighten and he snaps back into a straight-backed pose. His head is still bowed and eyes are still closed.

5 In the final stage his head snaps back to attention and he stands straight before the audience.

**SHYNESS**
One leg tucked in behind the other, hands clasped behind the back, head tilted, and eyes peeking up—all reveal his feelings of shyness.

**SURPRISE**
The puppet has his weight shifted back on one foot and his hands thrown up with the fingers spread wide. Add a small piece of polymer modeling clay to his face just under the nose, and make a small hole with the tip of a pencil. This open-mouthed expression, along with wide open eyes, should help to communicate surprise.

# Elaborate bow

The second bow creates a totally different performance. People really go to town bowing low, throwing one hand backward, often embellishing it with hand flourishes and kisses blown to the audience.

1 With one hand on his heart and the other thrown out to his side, the puppet fixes his gaze on his loving audience.

2 Use the blink technique as the puppet swoops forward, hand still on heart, one foot moving slightly ahead of the other.

3 In a dramatic gesture, the puppet's head falls heavily forward in gratitude for the audience's applause.

4 When the bow is complete, the puppet returns to his open, upright stance, arm outstretched.

## PRIDE
By throwing his chest out, placing his hand on his heart, and tilting his chin up, the puppet conveys pride to his audience. Observe people around you to see how body language reflects emotions.

## ANGER
Bring the puppet's shoulders up and back and flex the elbows. Bend the fingers and thumbs inward to form fists. Thrust the head and neck forward and down. Slanting eyelids and a down-turned mouth all contribute to an angry look. Magazine and newspaper photographs are great places to get angry expressions from as well.

# Puppet variations

Stop-motion puppets come in all shapes and sizes. They can be made using a range of techniques, from the low-cost, low-tech approach to very high-cost industrial processes such as silicone-casting and precision-engineered metal armatures.

*Using a basic wire armature base, you can make all kinds of puppets just by varying your clothing and finishing touches.*

## Making pin-down puppets

Puppets must be designed and built to be as lightweight as possible. The polymorph and wire armature is a very light construction, but by the time you have added the skinning material, clothes, and finishing touches, the finished puppet weighs a lot more than the armature and requires a tie-down system. The hare puppet pictured below is made in a slightly different way and is very light. Instead of glue and fabric, the shape of the rabbit is made by gluing and stitching hollow-fiber stuffing in place, then covering the whole thing in nylon. Hollow-fiber stuffing is the synthetic material found in cushions and comforters. A pair of pantyhose provides the fabric for the skin. This puppet is so light, in fact, that ordinary dressmakers' pins are enough to hold it firmly in place. These pins are then pushed into a sheet of cork or pinboard taped to the tabletop.

Finished hare with simple tie-down detail

**MAKING A PIN-DOWN PUPPET**

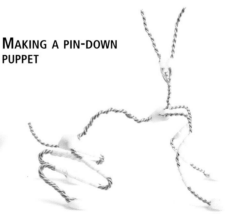

**TIP**
Make a sketch or two of the puppet you wish to make and research your character's anatomy. A few pictures and drawings can really help you to get the proportions correct and the joints in the right place.

1 The armature-making process is very similar to the one outlined on pages 72–75. Working from your sketches and research, bend your twisted wire into the shape of the hare. Include the head and ears. Add the polymorph bones on the sections you wish to remain rigid. As you're using pins as tie-downs there is no need to add the screw and nut to the feet.

2 Paint a thin layer of glue onto the armature and begin to add small amounts of the stuffing. You can begin to sculpt a rabbit shape at this stage. Hold the sections in place with basting stitches.

# Puppet design

The first few puppets you build will more than likely be used to test and practice your animation skills. However, once you have grasped the basics of puppetmaking and shooting in stop-motion, you may wish to animate a specific story or sequence. In this case, the design of your puppet will be very much influenced by two factors.

## WHAT TYPE OF FILM IS IT?

A puppet designed to perform a series of visual gags in a short comic sketch will look very different than an evil character designed for a dark folk tale. The story you are telling and the audience you are hoping to reach will help you decide on an aesthetic look for your puppet.

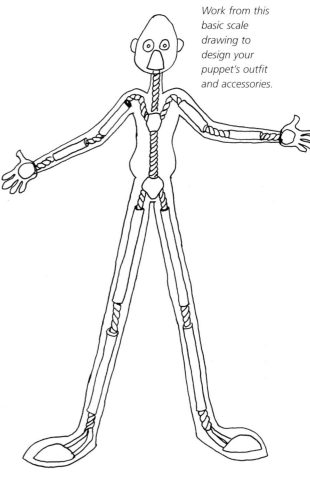

*Work from this basic scale drawing to design your puppet's outfit and accessories.*

## WHAT TYPE OF MOVEMENT IS THE PUPPET EXPECTED TO PERFORM?

A character that is required to walk or dance will wear out more quickly than a secondary character with fewer actions to perform. Be economical about characters that only appear briefly on the screen. Cut down on materials and time by shooting these puppets in close-up only, thus doing away with the need for legs and feet.

*The puppet pictured above was built for the seven-minute film Peacock, which took three months to shoot. In order to withstand the stress put on the puppet during such a long shoot, the armature underneath was built using ball-and-socket metal joints. These joints are specially made for the stop-motion animation industry, and a full ball-and-socket armature is very expensive to buy. The puppet's body and head were cast from a mold and made from silicone.*

*The puppets pictured here were designed and made by animator Rebecca Hurwitz. The armatures are made from twisted wire, and the bodies were made by building up layers of hollow-fiber stuffing and glue. The clothing is felt, glued, and stitched in place. These puppets are a perfect example of how expressive and charming a simple design can be.*

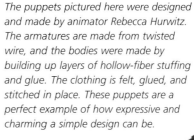

3 Cover the entire puppet in nylon, stretching it taut and holding it in place with small, neat stitches. Add facial detail.

*The finished puppet is simple, light, and flexible.*

# Making props and sets for stop-motion

As you become more confident with building stop-motion puppets, you may wish to shoot a more ambitious piece involving props or a set. Set building can be as complex or as simple as you like. Let's first take a look at some simple solutions to providing a background for your puppet.

## Simple background

The easiest way to provide your puppet with a simple and consistent background is to attach a sheet of paper or fabric to the wall behind the animation table. Drape the background material in a gentle curve down from the wall and over the surface of the stop-motion table.

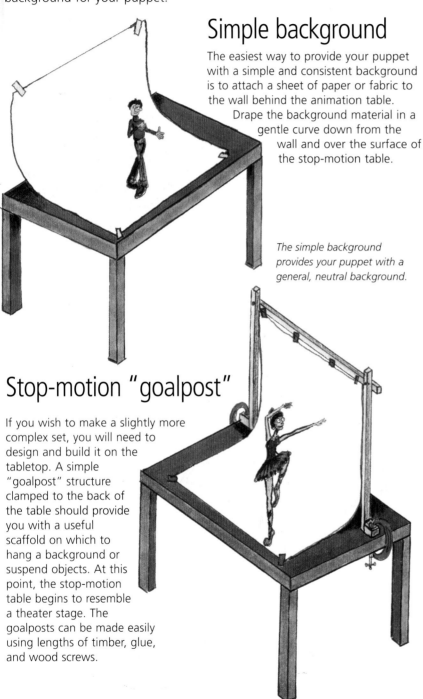

*The simple background provides your puppet with a general, neutral background.*

## Stop-motion "goalpost"

If you wish to make a slightly more complex set, you will need to design and build it on the tabletop. A simple "goalpost" structure clamped to the back of the table should provide you with a useful scaffold on which to hang a background or suspend objects. At this point, the stop-motion table begins to resemble a theater stage. The goalposts can be made easily using lengths of timber, glue, and wood screws.

*The goalpost background lets you get creative and introduce suspended elements against your backdrop.*

**Take your cue from your puppet**
There are some aesthetic rules that must be adhered to when designing sets. If your puppet is quite realistic looking, clay props and a set made from paper and card will make the puppet look less believable. Similarly, if your puppet is quite childlike, realistic furniture won't work well with it. Make a design decision based on the "look" of your sequence, on the puppet's design, and on the story.

**Keep it simple**
For an interior set show only the essentials. You do not need to build a dressing table, wardrobe, full-length mirror, clothes hamper, teddy bear, slippers, and chest of drawers if the film is based around a man in bed ignoring his alarm clock. Give your audience credit. They will figure out the setting in the first seconds of the piece, and then they just want to get involved in the story.

**Scale**
Be disciplined about the size of your puppets and sets. If the story requires the puppet to stand in the middle of a huge church, build a mini interior and a tiny puppet. Then, cut to a close-up against a generic background. If you are adding details such as wallpaper patterns or brickwork, put some effort into figuring out the correct scale for the size of puppet. If doorways and chairs are central to the plot, the puppet must measure up to them in human scale.

**Keep the action to the front of the set**
Remember that you will need to animate the puppet within your set. Placing an important feature—a doorway, for instance—in the middle of the back wall will result in you having to stretch ridiculously to animate the puppet walking through it. Remember, you can always just move the camera around the set.

**Positioning**
Everything in the set must be firmly fixed down— even items that may move during the scene. Sometimes when you are animating you need to access the puppet from an awkward angle, and you cannot avoid nudging objects. If anything shifts or falls over during shooting you will never get it back into the same position again (you will only waste a lot of time trying!)

# Useful materials for set building

**Paper**
*Little details, like pictures on walls or even curtains, can be drawn on paper, cut out, and glued onto the set.*

**Balsa wood**
*This lightweight wood is easy to cut and glue. It can be sanded and painted, and it works well if you need to make realistic tables, chairs, and doors.*

**Cardboard**
*While card is a little wobbly for walls and structural elements, it works well for smaller props, like this clock.*

**Foamcore**
*A lightweight, thin board that can be easily cut with a craft knife, you can use foamcore for walls, furniture (like this table), and flat props.*

**Polymer clay**
*Polymer clays can be modeled and baked to form small objects and props, like this telephone and fruit bowl. These work well aesthetically if your puppet's head is made of the same material.*

# Lights, camera,
# very slow action…

Good set design and appropriate materials will greatly enhance your production, but there are a few more elements that will make the world you have created come to life and engage the audience.

### Walls
Only use two walls for an interior set. You can easily access the puppets, and the camera can be placed in front of the set, or to the left, shooting from across the room.

### Surface details
Avoid the trap of becoming a miniature interior decorator. Plain walls and simple details will focus attention on the puppet.

### Keep it all flexible
Clamp the walls in place rather than fixing them down. It is useful to be able to shift a wall in order to make room for the camera or the animator.

### Lighting
Lighting a set can be challenging. You will get good results if you can control the intensity of the light, as well as the position. You might need to invest in some lamps that can be dimmed individually.

### Floor surface
A neutral floor surface, such as this wooden one, is perfect for hiding tie-down holes. Simply fill the holes with plasticine mixed to match the floor color. A few flecks of paint, mixed to the same color, give the floor a mottled appearance and hide the holes perfectly.

## STAGE LIGHTING FOR DRAMATIC EFFECT

Lighting the puppet is usually the first objective of stage lighting design—we light the puppet to make it visible and to help focus and direct the attention of the audience. A lighting area is nothing more than a single localized or confined space provided by one or more spotlights, so when lighting the puppet, the direction of light is very important from both a practical and dramatic point of view.

**Lighting and shadow**
If you can, try to light the set as if it were a real environment. For example, place a lamp outside a cut-out window shape in the set to create a natural shadow on the floor.

### Very low frontlight
*This will cause the puppet's shadow to increase in size and it gives a very unnatural look to the face. Although useful for dramatic effects, this angle is seldom used to light the puppet. Low frontlights (footlights, for example) help to reduce shadows from the overhead lighting if used at a lower intensity and as a "fill" light.*

### Backlight
*This does little to illuminate the face of the puppet but it can help separate the puppet from the background. As light does not fall directly on the puppet's face, strong colors are often used. Backlights may be used in any position: high, low, diagonal, and everything in between.*

### Sidelight
*This provides dramatic lighting to the side of the puppet and can often fill in shadows caused by front- or backlighting. Strong sidelight can also provide a sense of direction and motivation (sun, moon, warm, cool, etc.). Sidelight can add plasticity and a three-dimensional quality to the lighting (compared to low frontlighting) and is often used as a basic component when lighting the acting area.*

### Two sidelights
*These provide a nice confined lighting area, with interesting lighting to the face of the puppet and no spill upstage.*

### Downlight
*Illuminating a very confined area, downlight produces harsh shadows on the puppet's face. The angle may be useful for dance and dramatic lighting but is not helpful when the face requires good visibility.*

### Frontlight
*A frontlight (45–60 degrees) probably provides the best lighting to the puppet's face and eyes and allows an even greater range of movement (forward and back). Note, however, that the area is less confined and spills even further upstage.*

# Gallery: sets and props

Building sets and props for stop-motion requires huge amounts of imagination and innovation. The images below are still frames taken from six films. They represent only a small sample in terms of the range of materials that can be used in set and prop design for stop-motion. Each approach is unique and individual, and reflects the spirit of the piece, the tools and techniques available, and the designer's own creative vision.

**Tivish** *by Mary Murphy*

*The set here was simply painted onto a piece of hardboard, which was then hung against the wall. The moon is a circle of white paper with a spotlight trained onto it. The landscape was made from pieces of upholstery foam tucked under black cloth. Image one shows the full-sized puppet, but shot two is a miniature version of the same character, shot on the same set.*

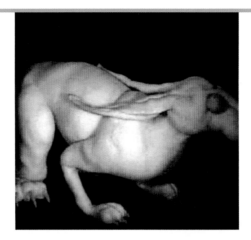

**Peacock** *by Mary Murphy*

*Found objects can sometimes work very well as props. The hairbrush on the dressing table in the first still is the head of a large toothbrush spray-painted gold. The picture frame started its life as a key ring, and the pot was a gift originally filled with perfume. The second still frame shows how a simple set allows the audience to focus on the puppet's performance. The backdrop is a black velvet curtain, which doesn't compete with the character for attention.*

**Hiking Trip** *by Cari Merryman*

*The trees in this set were very simply made. The tree trunks are made from bamboo covered with paper. The color and texture was achieved by printing a photograph of a tree trunk. The leaves were made in the same way, cut to various sizes, and glued into place.*

**Yoke** *by Mary Murphy*

*The sky was made by hanging a velvet cloth over a large lightbox turned on its side. The stars and moon are holes in the cloth. The landscape is made from upholstery foam covered in a stretchy fleece material. The egg was made by covering a balloon with layers of tissue paper and PVA glue.*

**The Mason** *by Vibeke Cleaverly*

*The walls of this naturalistic-looking set were constructed from particle board, and the logs were made with split dowling rods. The realistic furniture was made from balsa wood.*

**Sandcastles** *by Rebecca Hurwitz*

*Everything in this film was made using wire and felt. This film is an excellent illustration of how your choice of material for props and sets should be influenced by the design of your puppet and by the type of story being told. The charcters are in harmony with the set.*

 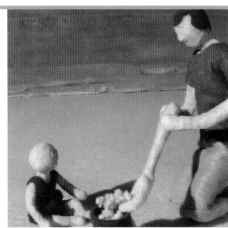

# Stop-motion animation sequences in camera

Always consider the puppet's part in the story and the movements they are meant to perform before starting a sequence, no matter how skilled you become with stop-motion animation. It's important to have a clear idea of where you want to begin and end your story. Stop-motion is not the best technique for improvisation.

## Yoga

This sequence demonstrates the importance of good tie-downs. In order to animate the puppet squatting down, a certain amount of downward pressure is required. To make it stand upright, it must be pulled upward gradually. This is made easier if the puppet is firmly fixed to the table.

# For you…

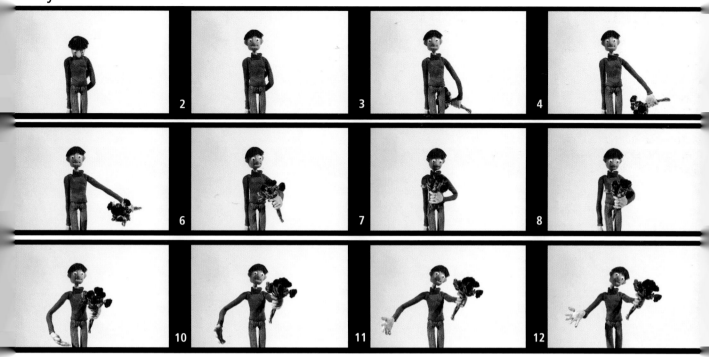

Performance is important when animating with puppets. It is the job of the animator to plan what the puppet will be doing, but a well-animated sequence should also convey what the puppet is thinking. The position of the head in the first frame lets the audience know that the character is shy about something.

# For me…?

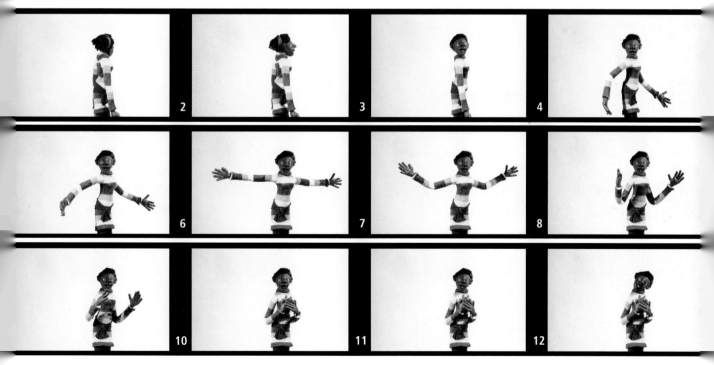

This sequence is a reaction to the actions of the character in the strip above. It could be edited to simply run directly after the sequence with the flowers, or both could be cut together to show her reaction to the flowers before his open-handed gesture.

# Making a **show reel**

As you work your way through the different projects in this book, you will build up quite a collection of clips and short tests. You can show this material to others in its raw state, but it is much more rewarding to produce a short sequence containing your best work, known as a "show reel." Putting your work together with music, effects, and titles is also a great way to introduce yourself to the technology and skills you will need in order to make a film.

## Getting your reel ready

To produce a show reel you need to use one of the editing programs discussed on page 13. It will take a little practice before you get to know your way around the editing package, but once you become familiar with the basic functions detailed over the next few pages, you can begin to edit your show reel together. The editing program used here is iMovies, but the steps are the same for any editing program (the interface will just look a little different).

### PICK CLIPS

1 Your show reel will be made up of animated clips exported from your capture program. Choose the clips you want to use, give each one an appropriate name, and save them all in one designated folder.

### IMPORT CLIPS

2 In your editing program, click on "file" and "import" to bring those clips into the program. They will upload into the "clip pane," or "clip viewer" on the left of the screen. This is essentially where all your animated sequences will be stored, ready for you to select and use.

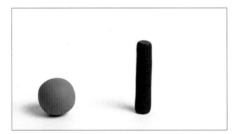

**Review your work**
*Only choose the best of your clips to appear in your show reel.*

**Clip pane**
In the clip pane you can see your pieces side by side, making it easier to choose an order.

### ELEMENTS OF A SHOW REEL
A simple show reel should contain four basic elements:
• your animated clips
• simple transitions
• sound
• titles (opening and closing, plus end credits)

## MOVE CLIPS TO THE TIMELINE

3 Across the bottom of the screen you will see the timeline. To build your clips into a show reel, drag them from the clip pane to the timeline, placing them in the order of your choice. Press the play button located just above the timeline and you will see the first rough edit of your show reel. You can rearrange the clips by simply dragging them onto the timeline.

## TRANSITIONS

4 Initially, all your clips will play in a basic sequence, cutting directly from one clip to the next. You can add a nice slow dissolve between two clips, or choose an interesting transition by clicking on the "editing" tab and selecting from the list. Click and drag the icon down onto the timeline, and place it between two clips to apply any transition.

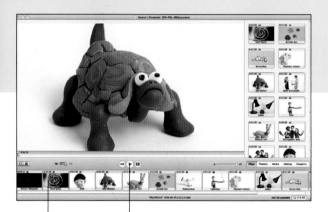

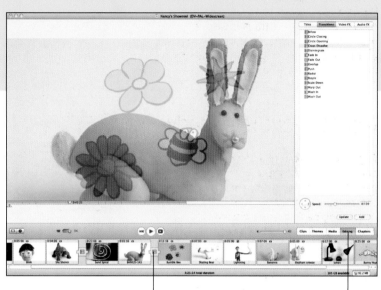

**Play button**
Watch your timeline in an animated sequence before making a decision.

**Timeline**
Examine your rough order on the visual timeline, then drag and drop clips to change the sequence order.

**Transition icon**
Once you've chosen your transition and dropped it on the timeline, it becomes visual.

**Editing tab**
Choose from a list of stock transitions to add interest between clips.

## Transition examples

*A "cross dissolve" starts with one clip...*

*...makes a ghostly transition where you are able to see both pieces together...*

*...and ends nicely in the second clip.*

*A "scale down" transition retains the image of the first clip...*

*...and simply causes it to recede into the distance...*

*...over the top of the second clip, which then replaces it.*

### SOUND

5 Just above the timeline, to the left of the screen, you will see two buttons. The button on the left will show your clips in the timeline. The button on the right will alter that view, showing the clips in relation to an audio timeline. Any sound clips you create or import will appear as purple strips on this audio line, and can be easily moved around.

### SPECIAL EFFECTS

6 In the editing window you will see a tab entitled "video FX." This window allows you to add a special effect to your clips, such as simple color adjustments and spectacular functions like "rain" and "earthquake." Simply click and drag to apply. Once you have tried a few effects, you can make a clip specially designed to work with the effects available. The "audio effects" tab in the same window allows you to add effects to your sound, such as "echo" and "reverb."

# Working with the software

## 3 QUICK WAYS TO ADD SOUND IN iMOVIES:

### • Add music from a CD or MP3 player
Use songs directly from a CD or your iTunes library. Select the song you wish to use, click on the "place at playhead" tab, and press play. The song will be directly recorded onto the timeline underneath your clips. Press stop when you have recorded what you need.

### • Add a sound effect in the audio window
You will find a range of prerecorded sound effects within the editing software. To add these to your project, simply drag them down to the timeline. Once they are there, you can place them anywhere you want to see how they work with your clips.

### • Record your voice with the built-in microphone
At the bottom of the audio window you will see a red button and the word "microphone." Click here to record your own voice directly onto the timeline. This function is very useful if you wish to record a voiceover or narration.

### QUICKTIME
Create a short clip to share with others by exporting your clips as a QuickTime movie with the touch of a couple of buttons. In iMovies, for example, go to the "file" menu and select "export." A window will appear with a range of export options laid out as tabs along the top. Select "QuickTime" and in the drop-down menu select the intended file type (for example, if you wish to send the film to someone via email, select the "email" option). Click the "share" button, and select a destination and name for your file. When the export is complete, simply attach this file to an e-mail, or burn a CD or a DVD.

### Video FX tab
Adding a lightning clip, like the one above, is easy—just choose from the list of your software's stock effects.

## TITLES

7 In the editing window you will see a tab marked "titles." Type in your desired title and select from a huge range of fonts, colors, and effects. For example, you can have the text bounce into frame, fly in letter by letter, or simply fade up from black. You can even set the title to appear over an animated clip.

## SHARING YOUR WORK

8 Now you have edited all your wonderful clips together and added music and titles. How do you get the reel out there to show your work to the world?

**Title tab**
Add effects to make the title of your reel come to life.

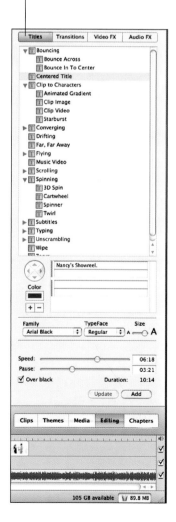

# Storing your reel

### KEEP AN ARCHIVED VERSION OF YOUR WORK

When you have completed your reel you will need to export it—the intended destination of the sequence will affect the export settings. Always export a full-quality digital copy for your own archive and save it with the individual clips. A digital copy is simply a full quality AVI or QuickTime file saved to the computer. This copy can be re-imported back into a new editing project in the future if you wish to use a section of the reel in another piece or if you want to add to the reel.

### FREE UP SOME SPACE

Animation files can lead to an overloaded hard drive. While making your show reel, export your clips to an external hard drive in order to free up more space on your computer. An external, portable hard drive is a great investment. Buy the largest storage space you can afford.

### THE INTERNET

It has never been simpler to post work on the internet. There are plenty of tutorials to guide you through putting your work on the net, and global websites such as YouTube are simple to use and a great way to get your work into the public domain.

### MAKE A CD OR DVD

If you keep the file size fairly small, you can export the film as a QuickTime or AVI file and simply copy to a standard CD, or burn a DVD if the file is larger. This disk will then play on any computer, or the file can be copied to the hard drive and played through QuickTime or Windows Media Player.

**CDs and DVDs**
*A portable way to show your reel*

**External hard drive**
*An indispensable piece of equipment for the animator*

# Making a **film**

Making a short animated film can be a hugely rewarding and very enjoyable experience. A wish to tell your own stories in your own way is one of the best reasons to become an animator. You can tell your story in a conventional way, or you can use a more experimental approach. Watch the work of other animators to discover the kind of animation you want to create. Every technique demonstrated in this book can potentially be used to make a film, but some stories are more suited to a specific technique. Look at the following four examples of animation techniques and the successful films they have made.

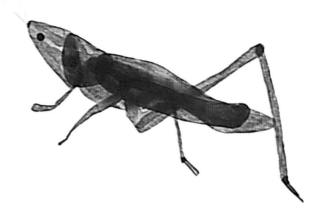

## Pixilation

Pixilation can be seen today in many music videos and even in feature films. The technique is most successsful when producing fast, quirky, and playful pieces. It's well suited to stories that blend live action with animated characters. In the series of film clips below we can see that a story using bright colors and quick movements—featuring, in this instance, eyes darting back and forth on socks, footless shoes dancing, and buttons with a will of their own—shows off the technique best.

*These frames are taken from the film* Best Fwends *by Libby Bass. Everyday objects such as shoes, clothing, and buttons are brought to life in this pixilated music video.*

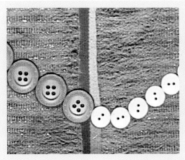

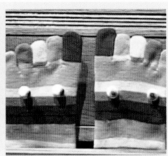

## Sand animation

Sand animations can be explorative, gentle, and abstract. The technique can create some of the most beautiful animated sequences with its extreme simplicity and its atmospheric qualities. On a lightbox, sand creates gorgeous silhouette images of dark on light, or the reverse. Well suited to illustrating timeless fables and legends, sand is a quiet, elegant medium that can also be made more complex by varying the thickness and distribution of the sand on the lightbox.

Yuji *by the Canadian animator Phillipe Vaucher demonstrates how effective and striking sand animation can be. By its nature, sand animation lends itself well to bold design.*

# Cut-out animation

Cut-out animation is a technique that is best used with action-oriented, or simple and childlike, stories. The characteristics of cut-outs mean that you can achieve some complex silhouettes and effects (such as the dart-like linear rain falling in the last image panel). Although you may be limited to telling your story on a flat plane, you can make your cut-outs as graphic as you like, with etching, decoration, and the use of shading.

*These beautiful jointed puppets were made for the film* Blossom *by Joy Chou. The characters are skillfully constructed in thin black card and rice paper, and the film was shot on a lightbox to create soft diffused colors and high-contrast figures.*

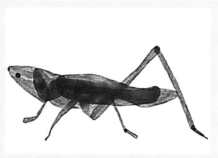   

# Stop-motion animation

Stop-motion animation can handle more complex storylines, plots, and detailed characterizations. One of the goals when using this technique is realistic movement. You can use many different types of materials with this technique, including clay, foam, latex, or an entire wire-armature covered puppet that has been designed with a couple of specific movements in mind.

*Sandcastles by Rebecca Hurwitz is a good example of how effective simple design for stop-motion can be. These basic characters are made entirely in one material—felt, and designed without eyes, mouths, or hands, yet they are endearing and tell their story with charm.*

## KEEP IT SIMPLE
Try not to bite off more than you can chew when planning your first film:
- Avoid dialogue or lip-sync (use a narrator off camera to tell the story).
- Quick visual jokes make good first films (adapt a nursery rhyme or an urban myth).
- Keep the duration to one minute or less, and don't be afraid to alter the script if it proves too difficult or time-consuming.

# Production cycle for making a film

### GENERATING AND DEVELOPING THE IDEA

1 At this point you should keep a small sketchbook of ideas, drawings, and pictures that inspire you. Watch lots of films, and keep two or three ideas simmering in your mind. When you find that you are thinking more about one of these ideas, put the others back on the shelf and move to the next stage.

### TREATMENT AND SCRIPT

2 A treatment is a written piece, outlining the key points of the film. A good treatment will focus on the mood and tone of the piece. Close your eyes and describe the film to a friend—this is your treatment. When you are done, ask the friend to describe the film. If the friend has no clue what kind of film you will be making, you may need to work a little more on the treatment. A script is really a more formal version of the treatment, indicating any narration, dialogue, and structure.

### STORYBOARD

3 A storyboard is essentially a series of drawn images and text that help you to visualize the finished film. It is a key tool in filmmaking that communicates a visual approach and helps the filmmakers "see" their films outside of their own imaginations.

### SCHEDULE

6 At this point you will begin to realize that the animator does not move the production cycle in a nice linear fashion. You may find yourself engaged in several of the processes at once, and it may become difficult to keep track of where you are in the production. A production schedule, with tasks clearly identified, is essential to keep your brain from exploding. Keep it on the wall by your capture station, and use a nice thick pen to check off tasks as they are completed.

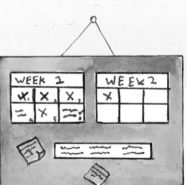

### CREATING THE ANIMATION

7 You will probably still be testing, and maybe even continuing work on the script and the storyboard, but you will know that you have reached this point when you begin to shoot frames of animation that will appear in the film.

### EDITING

8 You may edit while you are still shooting, but this phase begins with the storyboard. It gets underway when you import the animated clips into an editing package. Adding transitions, sound, and titles are all part of the editing process.

## DESIGN

4 The design stage is slightly different for every technique. If you are planning to make a cut-out piece, your design phase would involve planning and building your cut-out characters. You would also make your backgrounds and test the look of the piece under camera.

## TESTING

5 Even the most experienced animator will need to test his or her artwork. This is the point where you will find out just how challenging a task you have set yourself, and it is often during this phase that you will revisit your script or design to simplify or alter the narrative. The testing phase really continues throughout the production process.

## FORMATTING

9 Once your editing is complete, you will need to format your work according to the intended destination. This usually involves burning a DVD or making a digital file. If you are working to a deadline, it is important to understand that this process is never as simple as you think, and it can sometimes take a day or two to iron out all the kinks.

## DISTRIBUTION

10 This is the point where the recreational animator has a huge advantage over the professional filmmaker. You get to pick your audience. Some people will choose to show their work to friends and family. Others will post it up on a website and invite comment—there are a great many small film festivals out there that encourage new filmmakers. It is important to show your work, invite comment, and identify your own strengths and weaknesses as a filmmaker. Otherwise, how are you going to get that Oscar?

# Developing a storyboard:
# The Haunted House

Storyboarding is fundamental to the filmmaking process. The idea for this film came from a poem called, *The Haunted House*. Once you have an idea of your own, you will want to do some sketches and some brainstorming.

First, get a sense of the story and how you might want it to look. Then make some simple decisions. For this film, one decision was to have the poem read by a small child who would act as the film's narrator. Another decision was to use the technique of cut-out animation to tell the story. In order to stick to the simplicity of the poem, it was also decided that the whole film would be shot with few camera cuts and no camera moves.

Describe the action. It is useful to write a few descriptive lines about the story you will illustrate—a few background details and some information about the "look" of the piece should suffice. For example, the action centers on the image of a house against the backdrop of a beautiful summer's day. All the cut-out shapes are quite childlike, in keeping with the child's narration. A simple little tune will play at the start and end of the piece.

Sketch out your story. The drawings below are simple and quite rough, but you can see the visual elements of the film beginning to take shape. Remember that the storyboard is a

## MAKING A STORYBOARD

*Narrator: "The Haunted House"*
The camera fades up to a very simple house, made from cut-out shapes. The sky is blue, and there is a sun in the sky. The house is in the center of the frame, there are two large windows to either side of the front door, and there are puffs of smoke rising from the chimney. The yard is full of flowers.

*Narrator: "At night in the house . . ."*
One by one the windows turn black, the puffs of smoke vanish, and all the cheerful flowers sink down out of frame. With a creaky noise, the chimney leans to one side. A few loose stones tumble down from one of the windowsills and land on the ground.

*Narrator: "I hear a mouse."*
A mouse appears at one of the windows.

*Narrator: "(Maybe I should run and hide?)"*
The mouse starts to tremble and ducks down so only his eyes are peeping at the skeleton over the windowsill.

*Narrator: "I hear it again."*
The mouse pops back up and listens intently for a sound.

*Narrator: "Or is it the rain?"*
A rain shower appears in the frame, stops directly above the mouse, and starts to rain.

working document—just amend it if you want to make changes. At this stage, the film exists as ink and pencil lines on paper. Draw your storyboards on postcard-size paper rectangles traced from your animation field guide (see page 65), so you can swap them around and change elements easily. Write in a short description of each frame, and add in lines from the script.

*The Haunted House*

At night in the house, I hear a mouse.
Or is it a mouse, I hear in the house?
I think it's a ghost, a man that died.
(Maybe I should run and hide?)
I hear it again, or is it the rain?
Or a stone from a broken down wall...
But I think it's a mouse,
I hear in the house.
Not a ghost at all.

With a flourish, the mouse reveals a small trumpet, takes a huge, exaggerated breath, and brings the trumpet to his lips…

...but the narrator interrupts him.
*Narrator: "Or is it a mouse I hear in the house?"*
The mouse looks angry. He throws the trumpet away.

*Narrator: "I think it's a ghost, a man that died."*
In the other window, a skeleton in a top hat and bow tie appears. He grins and winks at the camera.

*Narrator: "Or a stone from the broken down wall?"*
A loose brick falls from the roof of the house and hits the mouse on the head.

*Narrator: "But I think it's a mouse, I hear in the house. Not a ghost at all."*
The mouse makes an angry "squeek!" to end the animation.

# Free stuff

Over the next few pages you'll find templates, plans, and blueprints to get you started on the different types of animation featured in this book. Jump in and try everything at least once to find out what techniques appeal to you.

## Cut-out templates for 2D animation

The templates here are the basic shapes used to make up the weightlifter (page 42) and the rabbit puppets (page 48). You can duplicate the patterns in three different ways:
- Trace the outlines onto plain white paper
- Photocopy the templates.
- Scan the image into your computer and print it out.

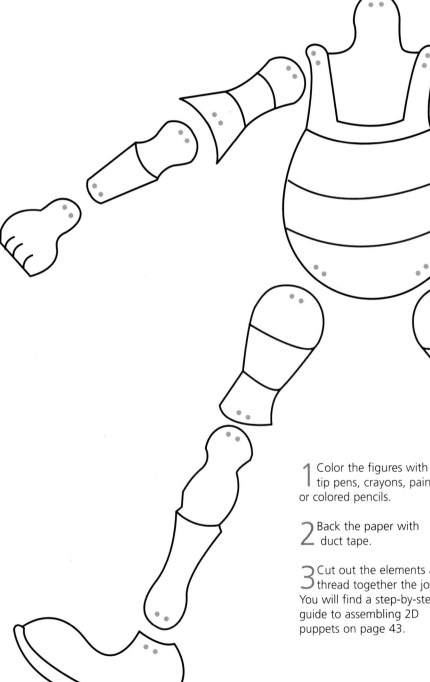

**The weightlifter**
*For possible colorways, see the working version of this puppet on page 42.*

1 Color the figures with felt-tip pens, crayons, paints, or colored pencils.

2 Back the paper with duct tape.

3 Cut out the elements and thread together the joints. You will find a step-by-step guide to assembling 2D puppets on page 43.

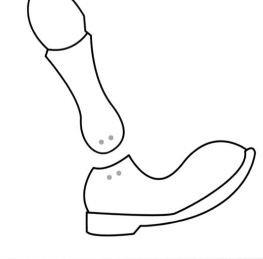

## The rabbit

The rabbit puppet is more complex than the weightlifter in the way it is strung together and how it moves. This template shows the basic structure of the puppet before stringing. Note the pairs of dots on each section. These indicate the best place to push the needle and thread through when joining the sections.

## How it moves

See how the sections overlap in the final puppet. This design lets the puppet extend its body and legs in a jump, but it also allows the figure to fold down into a more compact sitting position. This is achieved by allowing the sections (such as the head and upper body) to overlap and fold over each other.

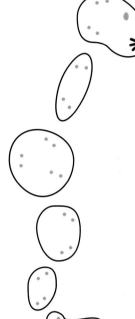
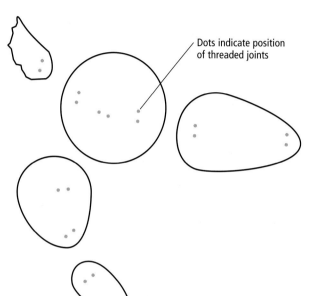

Dots indicate position of threaded joints

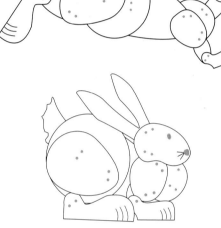

## 2D fish

As the fish are designed to be used in a replacement technique, there are no moving parts. Simply color the fish in, back the characters with duct tape, and cut them out. You will find more information on how to shoot replacement cut-out animation on page 50.

# Copystand and camera mount: plans and assembly

Making your own custom-built copystand and camera mount is a great way to keep costs down. Approximate measurements are suggested here, but as you will be making this to fit your own studio space, design it to whatever size suits you.

The easiest way to get the timber to the correct dimensions is to ask your hardware store; they will provide a cutting service for a very small charge.

## Tools needed

- electric drill with a set of drill bits in a range of sizes
- small screwdriver
- two small G-clamps
- Velcro bands or straps

The assembled stand

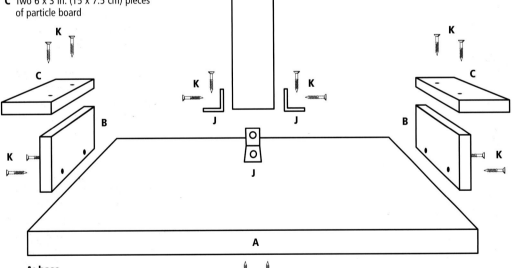

### D: center post
This forms the upright post in the center of the stand that will hold the camera mount. One 2 x 4 in. (5 x 10 cm) piece of timber (at least 25 in. [65 cm] long)

### B and C: sides
For the horizontal platforms on each side of the stand. Attach your adjustable clip-on lights here.

**B** Two 6 x 4 in. (15 x 10 cm) pieces of particle board
**C** Two 6 x 3 in. (15 x 7.5 cm) pieces of particle board

### A: base
Forms the flat base of the stand
One 22 x 17 in. (55 x 45 cm) rectangular particle board base, ½ in. (1.2 cm) thick

### H, I, J, and K: screws and brackets

**H** Two 2½–3 in. (6.5–7.5 cm) screws. Use these to attach the upright section to the base from underneath
**I** Six 1 1/16 in. (2.65 mm) screws. Use these to assemble the camera mount (see opposite)
**J** Three small right-angled metal brackets (at least 3 in. [7.5 cm] long on each side) to secure the center post to the base
**K** Fifteen 1¼–1½ in. (3–3.8 cm) screws to assemble and attach the sides and to attach the reinforcing brackets to the base and the upright section

## TO ASSEMBLE THE STAND

1 Assemble the sides first and attach them to the base. Take one section C and one section B, and form an inverted L shape.

2 Drill two small pilot holes, using a drill bit no bigger than the screws you have selected (a diameter of 3/16 in. [4.7 mm] is ideal).

3 Screw the section together tightly, and repeat with the remaining two sections C and B.

4 Again, drilling a small pilot hole first, attach the arms to the base (A), positioning them approximately halfway down the 17 in. (40 cm) length.

5 Position the center post (D) to the center back of the base, and secure using the right-angle brackets and the 1½ in. (3.8 cm) screws (K).

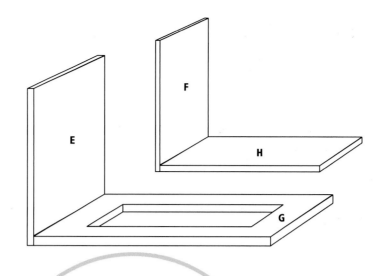

### E, F, G, and H: camera mount

These sections hold the camera in place and allow it to be secured at the desired height along the center post.

**E** One 4 x 6 in. (10 x 15 cm) rectangle, ⅛–¹⁄₁₆ in. (1.5–3mm) thick

**F** One 3 x 6 in. (7.5 x 15 cm) rectangle, ⅛–¹⁄₁₆ in. (1.5–3mm) thick
E and F form the upright section for both parts of the camera mount.

**G** One 4 x 8 in. (10 x 20 cm) rectangle, ⅛–¹⁄₁₆ in. (1.5–3mm) thick with cutout rectangular slot in the middle. This cut-out slot should run the length of the section and should be cut slightly wider than the lens of the camera you intend to use.

**H** One 4 x 3 in. (10 x 7.5 cm) rectangle, ⅛–¹⁄₁₆ in. (1.5–3mm) thick. This piece attaches to one of the rectangles from E and will form the L-shaped piece that will eventually be secured to the camera with the Velcro strips (see enlarged detail, right).

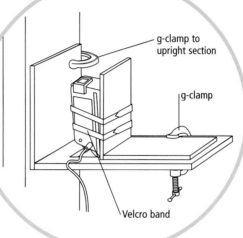

g-clamp to upright section

g-clamp

Velcro band

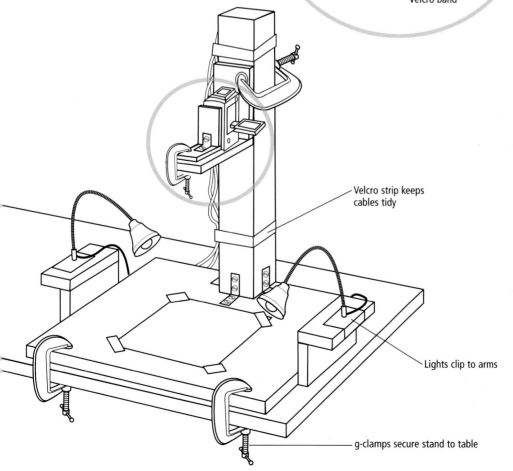

Velcro strip keeps cables tidy

Lights clip to arms

g-clamps secure stand to table

### TO ASSEMBLE THE CAMERA MOUNT

1 Using the smallest screws—not more than 1¹⁄₁₆ in. (2.65mm)—form two L-shaped sections using parts E, F, and G (as shown in the diagram).

2 If you are using a large or heavy camera, you may need to add metal brackets to reinforce the connection between parts E and F.

3 Secure the camera to the mount using Velcro bands and a small g-clamp. Clamp the entire section to the upright section as shown in the image, left.

4 When fully assembled, the stand should look like the image to the left. The lights are simply clipped to the platforms on each side. Use a pair of large g-clamps to secure the stand to the table. Keep cables tidy and out of your way by attaching them to the center post with a Velcro strap.

# Simple set design: templates

Pages 98–99 looked at ideas for sets. These two pages show two simple designs for an indoor and an outdoor set.

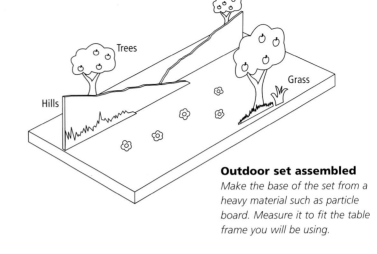

Trees

Hills

Grass

### Outdoor set assembled
*Make the base of the set from a heavy material such as particle board. Measure it to fit the table frame you will be using.*

### Outdoor set elements
*Trace off the trees, bushes, and hills onto foamcore, and cut them out using a craft knife. Color them by painting directly onto the surface or by gluing colored card or fabric onto the flat shapes.*

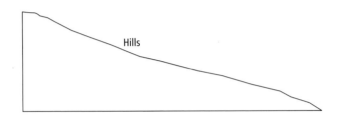

Hills

Grass

Tree

### Attaching the elements
*Because the flat elements are made from lightweight foamcore, they can easily be attached to the set using a small right-angled triangular brace. Attach one straight edge of the brace to the object using strips of tape or glue. Then, simply tape or glue the other edge to the set.*

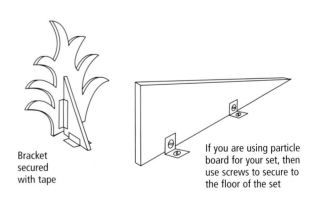

Bracket secured with tape

If you are using particle board for your set, then use screws to secure to the floor of the set

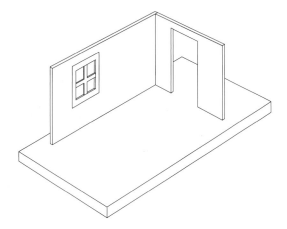

## Indoor set assembled

*An indoor set, like the one featured on page 99, can be built using the same technique as the outdoor version. You will need a heavy board to act as the base of the set.*

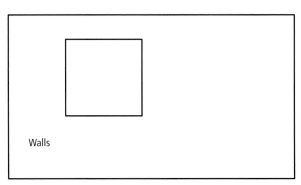

Walls

## Indoor set elements

*The basic set template consists of two walls: one with a door shape cut out and one with a window shape cut out. Use particle board instead of foamcore for the indoor set elements. Build the interior walls to the same scale as the puppet, and enlarge the templates using a photocopy machine.*

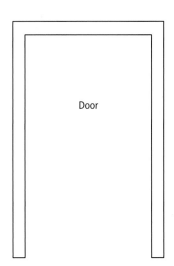

Door

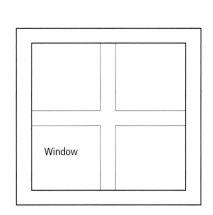

Window

## Door and window trim

*A baseboard along the bottom of the walls and a trim around the window and door adds visual detail and makes the set more interesting. Cut these out of foamcore and glue in place.*

## Brackets provide support

*Screw a series of small, right-angled brackets along the bottom edge of both walls, then screw the other side of each bracket into the set. Make sure that the screws you use are shorter than the thickness of the particle board, to avoid them poking through the other side. Once the basic set has been secured, dress it by adding details such as wallpaper, furniture, and so on.*

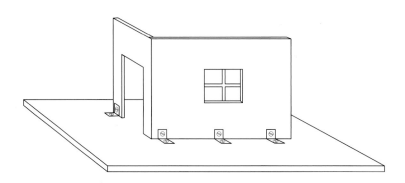

# Pattern for puppet's clothing

If your character is a very different size and shape to the one in the book (see pages 72–89), the pattern will need to be modified. In this case, consider this template as a starting point and use your puppet's dimensions to guide you.

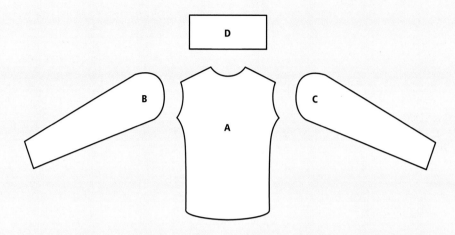

**A** front and back of the sweater, cut two
**B** left sleeve
**C** right sleeve
**D** turtleneck collar
**E** left leg of the jeans
**F** right leg of the jeans
**G** left turned-up cuff at the bottom of the leg
**H** right turned-up cuff at the bottom of the leg

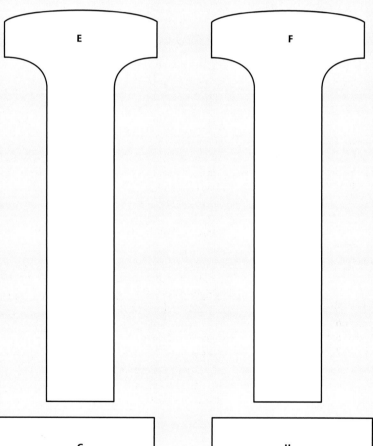

1 Trace the pattern shapes onto white paper and cut them out.

2 Attach the pattern pieces to the fabric of your choice, using dressmakers' pins, and cut them out.

3 Once you have cut your clothing pieces from the pattern, turn back to the project and follow the instructions for fitting the costume to the puppet.

# Resources

## Sand animation

### Lightboxes
Artograph
www.artograph.com
All kinds of lightboxes.

### Sand
The Colored Sand Company
www.coloredplaysand.com
White and colored sand.

### Paintbrushes
Blick Art Materials
www.dickblick.com

### Useful websites
National Film Board of Canada
www.nfb.ca
View the work of leading sand
animator, Caroline Leaf.

## Claymation

### Modeling clay
Van Aken
www.vanaken.com
A good-quality, non-hardening
modeling clay. See their store
locator for a retailer near you.

### Beads (for eyes)
BeadsRfun
www.beadsrfun.com
¼ in. (4 mm) round, pearl glass
beads.

### Useful websites
Clay Animation
www.clay.s5.com
An excellent site for clay
animators.

## Cut-out animation

### Colored paper
Mister Art
www.misterart.com
Hygloss bright color paper.

### Useful websites
YouTube
www.youtube.com
Watch *Miracle of Flight* by
Monty Python member and cut-
out animator Terry Gilliam.

www.youtube.com
Watch *The Overcoat* by the
award-winning Russian animator
Yuri Norstien.

## Pixilation animation

### Useful websites
Animation Network Television
www.awn.com

## 2D animation

### Round-pin peg bar
Lightfoot Animation Supplies
www.lightfootltd.com
Use with a standard hole punch.

### Basic 16:9 field-size guide
Animation Post
www.animationpost.co.uk
Download onto letter-size paper
by right-clicking the diagram on a
PC, or control + click on a Mac.

### Useful websites
Frank & Ollie
www.frankandollie.com
An excellent resource for the
novice 2D animator.

## Stop-motion animation

### Armature Wire
Blick Art Materials
www.dickblick.com
Aluminum armature wire in a
range of gauges and lengths.

### Polymorph
Kelvin
www.kelvin.com

### Very thin foam sheet
Pre-wrap
www.pre-wrap.com
Rolls of athletic pre-wrap foam.

### Useful websites
StopMotionAnimation
www.stopmotionanimation.com

Dark Strider
www.darkstrider.net
Have a look at the "tips, tricks,
& techniques" section.

## Set building and tools

### Particle board, brackets, screws
www.homedepot.com

## Animation software

### Stop Motion Pro
www.stopmotionpro.com
A software package designed for
use on a PC. It will work with a
miniDV and some stills cameras.

### FrameThief
www.framethief.com
A stop-motion capture program
for use on an Apple computer.

### iStopMotion
www.istopmotion.com
Another stop-motion program for
use on an Apple computer.

## Editing programs

### iMovie
www.apple.com/support/imovie
For a comprehensive tutorial on
how to use iMovie.

### Windows Movie Maker
www.microsoft.com/windowsxp
Search "moviemaker" for useful
tutorials.

### Useful websites
Animation World Network
www.awn.com
Online animation magazine.

Frames Per Second
www.fpsmagazine.com
Animation magazine.

## Animation books

*Stop Motion: Craft Skills for
Model Animation*
by Susannah Shaw
(Focal Press)

*The Encyclopedia of
Animation Techniques*
by Richard Taylor
(Book Sales)

*Animation: The Mechanics of
Motion*
by Chris Webster
(Focal Press)

*Cracking Animation: The
Aardman Book of 3-D
Animation*
by Peter Lord and Brian Sibley
(Harry N. Abrams, Inc.)

# Glossary

## Animation field size

Sometimes known as a "graticule," a field size is comprised of a series of standardized graded templates printed on paper or acetate. Each template holds the same ratio value (usually 16:9), and describes the shape of an animation frame in relation to the shape of the intended playback device such as a television screen.

## Anticipation

A small movement or a pause in the action that comes just before a more extreme movement. Anticipation helps to set up and punctuate the main action.

## Armature

The "skeleton" inside a stop-motion puppet. It allows the puppet to bend and move, while supporting the figure. Beginners will use twisted aluminum wire, but in the industry expensive ball-and-socket structures are often designed and built.

## Boil

Where a pause in the action can suspend the lively, hand-drawn look of a 2D sequence, a "boiling" look is achieved by cycling a number of nonmoving drawings. This boil keeps the line lively and is more in keeping with the type of line used when the subject is moving.

## Capture

To record a frame of animation and transfer it into a computer. In this book, capturing is done through the camera and transferred via a USB or firewire cable.

## Claymation

Stop-action animation using clay models.

## Conditioning the clay

The process of kneading a lump of clay between your hands to warm the material and mix the oil that makes the clay both soft and plastic.

## Copystand

A piece of studio furniture used for shooting flat artwork made of a flat heavy base, vertical center column, and camera mount.

## Core

In a stop-motion puppet, the central supporting and structural material, usually lightweight, and secured to the armature—for example, foam, polymorph.

## Cycle

A number of animated frames that are edited together several times in a seamless loop to extend a specific action. Cycling frames work best with a repeated consistent action, such as a bird flapping its wings.

## Drag

The movement of a secondary element in an animation sequence—for example, clothing, hair. The primary element (the head, for instance) will move from X to Y, and the hair will "drag" behind, taking a little time to accompany the head.

## Field guide

A punched sheet printed to indicate the sizes of all standard fields. When placed over an artwork, it indicates the area in which the animation takes place.

## Flip book

Simple animation made by drawing a series of images on the pages of a book and flipping through it with your thumb to make the characters or design move.

## Frame

One recorded image. Animation is shot at 29.5 frames per second.

## Frame rate

The number of frames per second at which a film is intended to be viewed.

## Lightbox
A box with a light in it. Animators use the light behind several sheets of paper in order to see several drawing layers at once.

## Line test
A process whereby a rough or unfinished series of drawings is recorded and played back to check the action before completing the sequence.

## Live-capture window
A facility built into most animation capture programs, it is a live version of the camera view incorporated into the software interface.

## Loop
Playing a sequence over and over with the last frame followed each time by the first.

## Onion Skin tool
A tool commonly found in the capture software that allows the animator to see a faint overlay of the previous frame superimposed on the live image. It assists in positioning the subject and in pacing the action while shooting.

## Peg bar
A small, flat strip of plastic with two or three upright pegs. It is used to register paper when drawing and recording traditional 2D animation.

## Peg bar punch
A professional paper punch, used to create a series of holes that slot over the holes in the peg bar.

## Registration
The exact alignment of various levels of artwork in precise relation to each other.

## Shooting in 2s
A commonly used animation process whereby every frame of animation is recorded twice, cutting down on shooting time. You shoot in twos by taking two shots every time you move or modify the image.

## Shooting a hold
Often used at the start and end of a simple sequence, shooting a hold involves recording a number of frames without moving or modifying the subject. This allows the viewer a few seconds to take in the subject before the animation begins. It can also be used in the middle of a sequence to help pace action.

## Skinning
The process of covering up the puppet armature with material to give shape and form to the character. Beginners usually work with upholstery, foam, glue, and fabric, but in the industry a range of more high-tech materials can be incorporated, such as resin, foam latex, and silicone.

## Stop-action or stop-motion
Animation where a model is moved incrementally and photographed one frame at a time.

## Storyboard
A series of still drawings that maps out a proposed story over a number of separate panels.

## Subject
The image or object being animated.

## Tie-down
A small screw-and-nut device built into the bottom of a stop-motion puppet's feet. It allows the model to be firmly attached to a tabletop.

# Index

# Credits

Quarto would like to thank the contributing animators for kindly supplying the film stills reproduced in this book.

Many artists are acknowledged beside their work. Other photographs and illustrations are the copyright of Quarto Publishing plc. While every effort has been made to credit contributors, Quarto would like to apologize should there have been any omissions or errors—and would be pleased to make the appropriate correction for future editions of the book.

# Author's acknowledgments

I would like to sincerely thank everyone at Quarto Publishing, and in particular Kate Kirby, Anna Plucinska, and Trisha Telep.

Thank you to John Urry for his patience, tolerance, and for his enormous contribution to this book. Thank you to Nancy, Eimer, Roseleen, Patricia, and Thomas Murphy for being on the other end of the telephone. Thanks also to Mike Brent, Chris Rydelski, Janet Mills, and Paul Jones.

Thanks to my friends, colleagues, and students at the University of the West of England in Bristol for their ongoing support and encouragement. A very heartfelt thanks to all the animators who allowed me to use screenshots of their work in the book—Libby Bass, Rebecca Hurwitz, Phillipe Vaucher, Ceri Merryman, and Joy Chou. Thank you to Vibeke Cleaverley for her contributions to the book, and for her invaluable assistance in shooting the animated sequences.

I would also like to acknowledge the contribution of five teachers who supported and encouraged me during my time as a student. For their patience, understanding, and intelligence, I'd like to thank Liam O'Byrne, Anne Brennan, Mary Morgan, Henry Pim, and Chris Webster.